T0380814

THE ANTI-SUICIDE BOOK FOR CHRISTIANS

Darnell L. Sherman MS AMFT

BALBOA.PRESS

A DIVISION OF HAY HOUSE

Balboa Press books may be ordered through booksellers or by contacting:

Balboa Press
A Division of Hay House
1663 Liberty Drive
Bloomington, IN 47403
www.balboapress.com
844-682-1282

Because of the dynamic nature of the Internet, any web addresses or links contained in this book may have changed since publication and may no longer be valid. The views expressed in this work are solely those of the author and do not necessarily reflect the views of the publisher, and the publisher hereby disclaims any responsibility for them.

The author of this book does not dispense medical advice or prescribe the use of any technique as a form of treatment for physical, emotional, or medical problems without the advice of a physician, either directly or indirectly. The intent of the author is only to offer information of a general nature to help you in your quest for emotional and spiritual well-being. In the event you use any of the information in this book for yourself, which is your constitutional right, the author and the publisher assume no responsibility for your actions.

Any people depicted in stock imagery provided by Getty Images are models, and such images are being used for illustrative purposes only.
Certain stock imagery © Getty Images.

Authorized (King James) Version (AKJV)
KJV reproduced by permission of Cambridge University Press, the Crown's patentee in the UK.

Print information available on the last page.

ISBN: 979-8-7652-4348-0 (sc)
ISBN: 979-8-7652-4347-3 (e)

Library of Congress Control Number: 2023911933

Balboa Press rev. date: 09/30/2023

For the abused and neglected children of the world.

<u>BLESSING</u>

Jesus Christ is Lord of all
Jesus Christ is Lord of all which was
Jesus Christ is Lord over all which is
Jesus Christ is Lord over all which shall be
Jesus Christ is Lord of all
God our Creator
Our world without end

Thou Shalt Not Kill. Exodus 20:13

CONTENTS

TEN REASONS NOT TO KILL YOURSELF

1. Jesus Christ is Lord. God made a conscious choice to create you and God loves you. God does not want you to hurt yourself. God could have created you at any time in human history, but God created you for such a time as this. God wants you to remain alive upon the earth for a specific purpose, until the day he calls you home. Our enemy the devil, wants you to hurt and kill yourself, don't give in to his prompts. Reject him in the name of Jesus Christ. We can prevail over the devil and all our enemies with the help of the Holy Spirit. God has all power and is almighty. Jesus Christ stated, he has all power in heaven and in earth; trust him, never give up, never commit suicide and choose life.

2. God is not ready for you to die yet, the time will come when you will leave this planet; however, the time is not now. It is inevitable that we shall all leave this planet sooner or later, but it is for God to determine when; not us.

3. God made you unique. In the entire universe there is only one you. No matter the hard times or the position you may find yourself in; remember you are unique and very special. You are God's creation. God has his majestic reasons for preserving your life on earth at this time. If you are unaware of your purpose in life, pray to God and ask him to help you discover it.

4. Despite the hard times you may be going through; if you place your faith and trust in Jesus Christ and pray for his help; you can be confident he will be there for you, and not abandon you. Jesus Christ can deliver and heal people suffering from broken hearts, poverty, homelessness, sadness, addictions, medical issues and mental health issues. Jesus Christ does provide significant meaning to our lives.

5. If you kill yourself, you risk a very good chance of burning in hell forever. Thou shalt not kill, is a commandment of God, which means we should not kill others; except in self-defense, nor should we kill ourselves. As painful as life can be in this material world, the pain and agony of hell is a trillion times worse. You don't want your last act upon the earth, to be murder and the rejection of human life, which God graciously visited upon you.

6. Your life is valuable. You are just as important as any other human being in the world, regardless of status. Despite those who may not see your worth or value, your life, journey and testimony are very important. Your story is not over yet; only the Lord

knows what great achievements await you, if you would only place your faith and trust in him, and not give up.

7. You have a great and powerful ability to positively affect the lives of others, even through a smile or an encouraging word. You still possess the ability to help others in ways you may not even realize. You can be a huge inspiration to others, by assisting them in overcoming their tragedy and trauma.

8. We all owe God a debt of gratitude, to value and honor the gifts of life and love he has visited upon us. Killing one's self would be dishonoring these precious gifts.

9. If you killed yourself, you would be severely hurting those who love you, and be providing a horrible example of how to cope with pain and difficulties.

10. Love yourself. See the good in yourself. See the positive, beautiful and wonderful qualities you possess. According to the World Population Review, approximately 160,000 people die daily around the world. God has protected your life all these years for a specific reason. You have survived thus far, because God wants you alive on the earth, for such a time as this. Life is not perfect on this planet, but it will be perfect in heaven. Through the hard times never give up, and through all situations in life, place your trust and faith in God, and he will see you through the hard times, to a glorious and majestic existence in heaven, eternally wrapped in the warmth and comfort of God's love.

CHOOSE LIFE

Do not kill yourself. Your life has value and meaning, even though you may not see it at this moment in time. Whatever the situation is in your life, it can improve. Tomorrow is a new day. Suicide is an eternal solution to a temporary problem. God loves you very much; he chose to create you and to protect your life thus far. You have life because of God. Have you ever done something in the past, and the second you did it, you knew it was a terrible mistake; you regretted it, and you experienced instant remorse; this is what suicide is, except it is an eternal mistake you cannot fix. There is no turning back from suicide, and you cannot fix it or make amends for it.

You can have a brighter future and a more successful life. If we have Jesus Christ in our lives, we have everything, no matter who has abandoned us, or what situation we find ourselves in. Jesus Christ promised to never leave or abandon us. He is there for you; reach out to him in prayer and ask him to help you. If you have given your life to Jesus Christ, you are one with him, and the Holy Spirit lives within you. God wants you to live, and he will assist you in overcoming this difficult time in your life. Seek God; he is there for you. According to the world Population Review approximately 160,000 people die daily; God has kept you and allowed you to live through all of your years to this point in time, because he loves you, and he wants you to remain living on earth. There is a very important reason God created you in the first place. God did not have to create you; however, he chose to create you, because he loves you dearly, and he wanted you to be his son or daughter.

God has a reason for your life; you are important. If you were not meant to be here, you would have already died, or you would have never been born. God has a plan and purpose for your existence. Even if you are in a coma, or in an iron lung and can only wiggle a finger; your life can still make a positive and significant difference in the lives of others. If you ask God, he can and will forgive your sins. Despite the circumstances of your life, God loves you and wants you alive upon the earth, for such a time as this; (Esther 4:14). Choose life and not death. Embrace the love, meaning and purpose God has for your life.

Eventually, we all leave this planet; however, it is God's choice when we die; not ours. Whatever amount of time you have left on the earth, try to make the best of it while you are here, and follow the will of God for your life. If you don't know what the will of God is for your life, ask him and he will reveal it to you.

I know of what I speak. There was a time when I wanted to kill myself; I was angry and hurt. I was betrayed by someone I trusted to protect me and help me, and instead I was physically and emotionally abused by the individual, and then emotionally abused by another individual I trusted and sought help from. The reason, I did not kill myself was because I prayed to God and called on Jesus Christ for help. The Holy Spirit brought to my remembrance, Martin Luther King Jr., and the noble principles and values he lived for; he valued and promoted peace, justice and freedom. In a peaceful manner he sought to defeat oppression, racism and discrimination, and it cost him his life. The Holy Spirit told me to value life, and to live my life in a noble and just manner, and not to surrender my life because of sadness, sorrow and pain.

I am so grateful for the Holy Spirit ministering to me, during my times of personal crisis. I am overjoyed I made the choice not to kill myself. The Holy Spirit continues to help me overcome various moments of crisis in my life. I've learned to have lower expectations for human beings, and to only trust God 100%. I know God will never betray me, beat me or emotionally abuse me. You can count on God too!

Jesus Christ loves you. Though we may never meet on earth; I hope we will meet in heaven one day. Remember, *"Thou shalt not kill (Exodus 20:13)"*, is a commandment of God, and you cannot receive forgiveness once you are dead.

Live, embrace a relationship with God; feel and experience his love. Embrace faith and the promises of God. One day you will be in heaven with the Lord for all of eternity, if you simply trust and obey him. Through the hard times never give up! I love you. May Christ bless and keep you!

> *For God so loved the world, that he gave his only begotten Son, that whosoever believeth in him should not perish, but have everlasting life. John 3:16*

> *For if thou altogether holdest thy peace at this time, then shall there enlargement and deliverance arise to the Jews from another place; but thou and thy father's house shall be destroyed: and who knoweth whether thou art come to the kingdom for such a time as this? Esther 4:14*

In the event, you have not been born again through the precious blood of our Lord and Savior; Jesus Christ, you may accept him as your Lord and Savior, by honestly praying the following prayer. If you do this; your life will change for the better, and it will never be the same. Jesus Christ loves you.

> *Heavenly Father, I am a sinner; I repent of my sins. I now, accept Jesus Christ as the Lord and Savior of my life. Heavenly Father help me to become the person you want me to be. Thank you for saving me; in the precious name of Jesus Christ I pray, amen.*

CHOICES AND PURPOSE

Ideally and practically we should identify and seek a final purpose for our lives; an end goal if you will, an ultimate reason as to why we are living our lives. Let's use Johnny a high school student for example; perhaps Johnny's final purpose is to become a medical doctor. He has made a choice to become a medical doctor first and foremost. Understanding what careers are available to him is the first step. Attaining a general sense of what medical doctors do is another step in this process. Coming to a realization that he would like to perform the tasks of a medical doctor, is another step in the process. Attaining a general understanding of the requirements to become a medical doctor is another step in the process. Attaining the confidence that he has the ability to meet the requirements to become a medical doctor, is another step in the process.

The daily purpose for Johnny becomes to study, be disciplined and to attain good grades to enter into college and subsequently medical school. The final purpose for Johnny dictates his daily purpose for living. Johnny chooses to attend class daily, to study and earn good grades, which subsequently requires Johnny to lead a healthy existence and to be disciplined. Instead of sleeping until noon, Johnny awakens at 07:00 AM to be on time for his 08:30 AM biology class. The purpose of Johnny's life on this particular day is to promptly attend his 08:30 AM biology class, and to perform well in it. Johnny's final purpose necessitates lesser daily purposes to be attained, in order to attain the final purpose. In order for Johnny to become a medical doctor, he must do certain things, and he also must avoid doing certain things, which would disqualify him from becoming a medical doctor.

The final purpose I have identified for my life, is to go to heaven when I leave this planet, as a result there are certain choices I must make daily in order to attain my final purpose.

I have to understand how to attain my final purpose for my existence. I have to make the following choices to attain my final purpose; accept Jesus Christ as my Lord and Savior, and follow the Word of God, as expressed in the Holy Bible; in addition I have to follow the guidance of the Holy Spirit.

Jesus Christ requires his children to do certain things, and to avoid doing certain things. For instance, Jesus Christ requires me to love God, myself and others, including my enemies. Jesus Christ requires me to be truthful and merciful. Jesus Christ wants me to avoid committing adultery, bank robbery, lying, seeking revenge, and a whole host of other behaviors including committing suicide. Jesus Christ requires that not only my behavior be transformed from evil to his righteousness, but that my heart and soul be transformed from evil to his righteousness.

My daily purpose for living is dictated by my final purpose for living. For instance today, my purpose is to work on this manuscript, to pray, read the Holy Bible and communicate with others regarding the gospel of Jesus Christ. I believe these are activities God wants me to engage in today. Conversely; today, I do not plan to renounce my faith in Jesus Christ and become a Buddhist; neither do I plan to pick up a woman in a bar and have sex with her; these are activities which God does not want me to engage in, and the list goes on.

Earlier in my life, I had a purpose of becoming a psychotherapist, and by the grace of God, I achieved that purpose, but that was not my final purpose. It was a step towards my final purpose, because God wants humans to love and help each other. I believe, I help others by being a competent and caring psychotherapist. A good psychotherapist attempts to develop a psychologically intimate and trusting relationship with their clients, in order to assist them in living healthier and more successful lives. Simply, I chose to become a psychotherapist because I want to help people. Jesus Christ helped the whole world, and I am simply trying to follow in his footsteps on an obviously much, much lesser scale. Obviously, I cannot save someone's soul from eternal condemnation, but I can direct them to someone who can; Jesus Christ.

Everyone's final purpose should be to enter heaven when they leave the earth. One can become the greatest psychotherapist, basketball player, musician, poet and end up burning in hell forever.

> For what shall it profit a man, if he shall gain the whole world, and lose his own soul? Mark 8:36

Material success, the adulation and validation of man and fleshly pleasures ends at death; a relationship with Jesus Christ is eternal; heaven is eternal. Make heaven your final purpose. Make heaven your goal, and there is only one way to reach it.

> Jesus saith unto him, I am the way, the truth, and the life: no man cometh unto the Father, but by me. John 14:6

GOD LOVES AND STRENGTHENS US

The National Suicide Hotline in the United States is (telephone) 988 or (text) 741741, it is a 24 hour 7 days a week service. In the appendix there are other counseling resources listed. There is nothing wrong in seeking quality counseling if you are depressed, sad or simply need someone to talk to. We are helpers of each other.

Through tragic and hard times in life never give up. In all circumstances and situations in life, trust in our Lord and Savior, Jesus Christ, and rely upon the Holy Spirit to guide you through to a better day, and to eventual eternal life in heaven. Never commit suicide; do not kill yourself. Jesus Christ knows your pain and sorrow, and he loves you and cares about you greatly. The prophet Isaiah wrote of Jesus Christ:

> *He is despised and rejected of men; a man of sorrows, and acquainted with grief: and we hid as it were our faces from him; he was despised, and we esteemed him not. Surely he hath borne our griefs, and carried our sorrows: yet we did esteem him stricken, smitten of God, and afflicted. Isaiah 53:3-4*

This mortal existence is temporal, it will not last forever. You will either die, or be caught up in the rapture of the church of Jesus Christ. You are very important, regardless of who does not acknowledge your importance. You are important to God, as he chose to create you for a specific purpose. God has his reasons for what he does and allows in this material world. We may not know the reasons, but God did not make a mistake in creating you and allowing you to live to this point. God has preserved your life. Everyday on this planet, an average of approximately 160,000 people die according to the World Population Review. God has purposefully preserved your life up to this point, because he loves you, and wants you alive upon the earth for such a time as this.

You are a very valuable and important human being. You are unique and special; there is no one else like you in all of the universe. This time and space we are living in is unique. We need to value the moment, no matter what we are experiencing. There will never be a moment in time like this again; there will never be another you again. You are a unique person living in a unique time, for a specific purpose; embrace your life and time. You are a unique masterpiece of the greatest artist of all time; Jesus Christ. God does not make mistakes. God loves you and wanted you to exist, which is why he created you. God wants an intimate and affectionate relationship with you. God wants you to know how much he loves you, and he wants you to love him. I initially accepted Jesus Christ, as my Lord and Savior because I feared going to hell; however, over the years I experienced God's majestic love for me, and I learned to love God, and it has been the number one best experience of my life, and it has provided my life with infinite meaning and purpose beyond my wildest imagination.

As believers in Jesus Christ, we will not experience suffering in heaven. This time on earth, is the only time we will experience suffering. Don't be afraid of suffering; Jesus Christ was a man of sorrows and he was acquainted with grief; he knows intimately what you are going through. The Holy Spirit, Jesus Christ and the Heavenly Father are present to assist you through your pain, sorrow and misery. Turn to God and ask him for help, he will hear you and help you. Love God and trust God. Love yourself and love your fellow human beings.

Humans are not young and vibrant forever, a time comes when we all leave this planet. One of the exciting aspects of life; is that we never know when we will leave this planet. This is one of the reasons our hearts should always be right with God. There is a time when God will end our time on earth. It is only for God to determine when we are born, and when we leave this planet, because obviously God knows best.

Thou shalt not kill. Exodus 20:13

Once we are dead, we cannot repent of the sins we committed on earth. Heaven is much better than hell; a huge understatement. I am not God, so I cannot say who is in heaven and hell; however, just based on the word of God, we can know certain facts. One, it is a sin to kill. Two; therefore, it is a sin to kill one's self. Three, no matter the circumstances we find ourselves in, we should trust our Lord and Savior, Jesus Christ, and never give up.

Trust in the LORD with all thine heart; and lean not unto thine own understanding. In all thy ways acknowledge him, and he shall direct thy paths. Be not wise in thine own eyes: fear the LORD, and depart from evil. Proverbs 3:5-7

Many are the afflictions of the righteous: but the LORD delivereth him out of them all. Psalm 34:19

Jesus Christ is Lord. Long spiked nails, were hammered through his hands, and he was brutally beaten, and scourged with whips laced with jagged metal. He was pierced with a spear in his side, and a crown of thorns was violently pressed into his head. Jesus Christ was a blessing to every human he ever met. He healed the sick, and restored psychological, spiritual and physical health to many. Jesus Christ restored life, and he can restore life today. Jesus Christ

DARNELL L. SHERMAN MS AMFT

fed the hungry, forgave the guilty, and taught people the commandments of God. Jesus Christ is alive today, and he loves you dearly. Jesus Christ is the truth, the life and the only way to heaven.

When Jesus Christ lived physically upon the earth, many politicians and members of the religious hierarchy made vicious and false allegations against him; they also wickedly conspired to put him to death. Jesus Christ was crucified and died, and through the power of God, he was triumphantly resurrected three days after his death. Jesus Christ bared the sins of the whole world. Jesus Christ paid the price for the sins of all of humanity past, present and future. For anyone who accepts him as Lord and Savior of their life; he or she will go to heaven and not be eternally condemned to hell. For those who have placed their trust in Jesus Christ, they will spend eternity in heaven experiencing the pleasures, love and peace of God. A rest is coming to the children of God.

To accept Jesus Christ, as your Lord and Savior, pray the following prayer with sincerity:

> *"Heavenly Father, I thank you for hearing my prayer. I ask that you forgive me of my sins, and I surrender my life to you; I accept your son; Jesus Christ, as my Lord and Savior. I thank you for saving me and loving me. Please help and protect me, in the name of Jesus Christ I pray, amen."*

If you sincerely prayed the above prayer, you are saved. Your life will never be the same. Read the Holy Bible, pray everyday, try not to sin; however, if you sin, ask God to forgive you, and he will. Ask God to lead you to a Bible believing church, where you may hear the Word of God correctly taught, and build healthy relationships with your brothers and sisters in Jesus Christ.

No one lives forever on planet earth; our lives on this planet are temporary. The truth is not always a pleasant thing, but truth exists. Death is not a subjective, perceived truth; rather it is a universal truth which only the delusional deny. There are no two-hundred year old humans walking around on planet earth, because death is a reality; perhaps, not a pleasant reality, but a reality nonetheless. There is no need to kill one's self, we will all leave this planet soon enough. There is no need to rush the inevitable.

According to the Oxford Language Dictionary (2022), the definition of Nihilism is as follows: *The rejection of all religious and moral principles, in the belief that life is meaningless.* Organizations and individuals, who adhere to a nihilistic philosophy, would rarely admit that they are actually nihilists. They exist in every facet of our society, and the majority of nihilists are unaware that they are by definition nihilists. Regrettably, there is a tragic trend in the world of many adopting and putting Nihilism into practice; hence, the rise in suicide, murder, theft, substance abuse, sexually transmitted diseases, divorce, psychological disorders and overall immorality.

In subtle ways nihilistic politicians seek to decriminalize heinous acts such as murder, assault, battery, rape, child abuse and the use of destructive and addictive drugs. Nihilistic individuals seek to violate the rights of others, by choosing to rob, steal, kill, destroy property, extort, rape and terrorize. The majority of nihilists are atheists, who do not believe in God, or in any form of reward or punishment after death, such as heaven or hell.

America is a democracy (ruled by the majority); however, America seems to be slowly becoming an oligarchy (ruled by the few). What of suffering, pain, loneliness, a life with no meaning or purpose, and the realization of nothingness? What of a life immersed in the dialectic of Nihilism, which states, there is no God, no truth, no justice and there is no meaning or purpose in life.

Nihilists do whatever pleases them. Doing whatever pleases the individual, is becoming the mantra and philosophy of our present world order, and judges and politicians are changing laws to accommodate this mindset. It is a self-destructive philosophy. Such a philosophy has no regard for the sanctity of human life, or for the rights of other human beings. Most importantly, Nihilism has no regard for the Word of God.

> *This know also, that in the last days perilous times shall come. For men shall be lovers of their own selves, covetous, boasters, proud, blasphemers, disobedient to parents, unthankful, unholy, without natural affection, trucebreakers, false accusers, incontinent, fierce, despisers of those that are good, traitors, heady, high-minded, lovers of pleasures more than lovers of God; having a form of godliness, but denying the power thereof: from such turn away. II Timothy 3:1-5*

As long as I am on earth, I will be faced with temptation to sin; to violate the law of God. It is a struggle I would be rid of, if I could without violating any other law of God. Should I fantasize about a gorgeous woman I'm attracted to in the supermarket, and attempt to seduce her? Should I simply say a silent prayer for her and move on? Should I attempt to initiate a conversation with her, and if she is single invite her to an evening dinner? In this scenario I have a choice to make. God has visited free will upon me to make such a choice.

One day when I arrive in heaven, my struggle with temptation will be over. I long for that day, but I will not foolishly kill myself in an attempt to get to heaven quicker. I believe, if I killed myself I would go to hell. If I killed myself, I would have rejected the gift of existence and the life God chose to bestow upon me. If I killed myself, I could not seek forgiveness from God after I'm dead; therefore, my last willful act upon the earth would have been the murder of myself. If I jumped off a hundred story building, is it possible, I could experience remorse and ask God to forgive me as I'm falling, and before I smash into the ground? Perhaps, it is possible and perhaps God would forgive me; however, that is a chance I would never take. I also have a spiritual enemy the devil, who may try to inhibit my prayer as I was falling. The intensity of falling may be so intense, I could not manage to repent and ask God to forgive me. For those who have committed suicide, I do not know who was able to repent of their sins in their last few waning moments of life. I am not suggesting that everyone who ever committed suicide is burning in hell, because again they could have repented in their few waning moments of life. What I am saying is that, suicide is a rejection of the life and love our Heavenly Father chose to visit upon us. Suicide is also a sin, and one cannot repent of sin once one dies. Anyone who commits suicide is taking an unwise and very dangerous risk of being eternally condemned to hell forever, because they are not trusting God to help them through their pain and sorrow.

Whatever problems one may be facing on earth; the problems in hell will be a million times more painful. There is no escape from hell and the lake of fire; it is everlasting torment and agony. We know either death or the rapture is coming at some point in time, which for Christians will offer an eternal relief to our pain, struggle, temptation, loneliness, agony and sorrow. Jesus Christ has saved us and will rescue us; trust in him through the hard times and never commit suicide.

> *My son, forget not my law; but let thine heart keep my commandments: For length of days, and long life, and peace, shall they add to thee. Let not mercy and truth forsake thee: bind them about thy neck; write them upon the table of thine heart: So shalt thou find favour and good understanding in the sight of God and man. Trust in the LORD with all thine heart; and lean not unto thine own understanding. In all thy ways acknowledge him, and he shall direct thy paths. Be not wise in thine own eyes: fear the LORD, and depart from evil. Proverbs 3:1-7*

Trust in the Lord with all your heart, and lean not unto your own understanding. Trust in Jesus Christ; call upon him for help, feel his presence in your life, he will never leave you or forsake you. Our Heavenly Father understands the pain, sorrow and difficulty you may be experiencing; you are not alone. You are unique, you are special and you are God's child; he loves you more than you know; simply trust him and choose not to harm yourself.

Not to be naïve, I must admit there is an attraction to the do whatever pleases you. If I did not give my life to Jesus Christ; perhaps, I would have found temporary happiness and pleasure, in having sex with every beautiful woman I could convince to go to bed with me. Perhaps, I would have also found pleasure and satisfaction in seeking personal revenge on my enemies.

A few of the possible outcomes of indulging my sexual desires could have been, unwanted pregnancies resulting in children growing up without a father, or possibly children being murdered through abortion. I could have contracted and spread sexually transmitted diseases. I could have exploited women for my own selfish desires, and committed adultery and fornication, which could have led to countless tragedies.

A few of the possible outcomes of indulging my desire for vengeance could have been, murdering or injuring innocent people. I could have been killed in the process of attempting to exact vengeance. I could have been arrested and sentenced to the death penalty. I would have to face the consequences of not forgiving my enemies. I would have experienced guilt, remorse and regret. The ultimate and worst punishment of all, I could have been condemned to eternal condemnation in the lake of fire, by God.

I don't know the pain that Jesus Christ experienced. I don't know if my mind could even come close, to imagining what the pain and agony was like for Jesus Christ.

I have sinned in my life. I have committed evil acts in my life, and when I have been punished for them, I recall feeling that the punishment was not fair, and that it was too much. I don't like suffering and pain, yet in the back of my mind, I knew that I had done something wrong, and I was responsible for the painful consequences of my actions. In retrospect, looking back I believe all of the punishments I received from God were just, merciful and eventually benefited me. I am by no means perfect; however, I am not the sinner I used to be. By the Grace of God, I no longer commit some of the sins I used to indulge in. God revealed to me how harmful and self-destructive they were to others and to myself.

> *My son, despise not the chastening of the LORD; neither be weary of his correction: For whom the LORD loveth he correcteth; even as a father the son in whom he delighteth. Proverbs 3:11-12*

Jesus Christ never did anything wrong, and he was punished worse than any human being in history. How did Jesus Christ feel, knowing that he did not deserve any of the violence, agony, pain and condemnation he was suffering? I cannot imagine. Jesus Christ loved his Heavenly Father. The Heavenly Father loved Jesus Christ as well. They were one, yet Jesus Christ asked the Heavenly Father, why have you forsaken me? What a very emotionally painful moment that must have been for him. Yet, out of love, Jesus Christ chose to experience all of the aforementioned, agony, pain, suffering, ridicule, false accusations and heartache, in order that you and I may be saved from eternal condemnation, and experience the love, peace and protection of God for all of eternity.

> *For God so loved the world, that he gave his only begotten Son, that whosoever believeth on him, should not perish, but have everlasting life. John 3:16*

Suicide: The act or an instance of taking one's own life voluntarily and intentionally. Merriam-Webster (2022).

According to the Center for Disease Control and Prevention (CDC), in 2022, there were a total of 49,449 successful suicide attempts reported in America. The CDC reported in 2020, there were a total of 45,799 records of successful suicides in America. The CDC also reports that from 1999 through 2018, there has been a 35% increase in the records of suicides in America. According to the World Health Organization, there are approximately over 700,000 suicides reported worldwide annually.

> *The thief cometh not, but for to steal, and to kill, and to destroy: I am come that they might have life, and that they might have it more abundantly. John 10:10*

Jesus Christ spoke the aforementioned words. Jesus Christ wants us to experience life, and to experience life more abundantly. Experiencing life more abundantly does not necessarily mean being in possession of money or material resources. One may experience life abundantly living in a cardboard box under a bridge, being incarcerated in a prison, or living in a Newport Beach mansion. Abundant living incorporates being at peace with God, being guided by the Holy Spirit, and choosing to find one's meaning and purpose in life through Jesus Christ. John the Baptist had an abundant life, even though he wore camel's hair, a leather belt, and he ate locust and wild honey. John the Baptist, baptized our Lord and Savior, Jesus Christ. At the order of King; Herod Antipas, John the Baptist was unjustly beheaded. Herodias and her daughter, Salome conspired against John the Baptist to have him beheaded, because he told the king, he should not be sleeping with his brother's wife, Herodias. John the Baptist experienced a more abundant life, even though he was murdered young by beheading.

We will never find a perfect life in this material world. No matter how rich or poor, there will always be problems. The question becomes, do we allow the problems to defeat us, or do we through the power of the Holy Spirit overcome the problems and follow the will of God for our lives.

> *Jesus answered and said unto him, Verily, verily, I say unto thee, except a man be born again, he cannot see the kingdom of God. John 3:3*

Jesus said we must be born again, if we are to enter heaven. The process begins when one accepts Jesus Christ, as their Lord and Savior. To accept Jesus Christ, as one's Lord and Savior, the individual begins to surrender their will to God, in acknowledging that they cannot save themselves, and that they are in need of a Savior for various reasons. One reason is to save their immortal soul from hell and eternal condemnation. Another reason is to bring a significant meaning and purpose to their life. Another reason is to enter into a mutual, trusting and loving relationship with one's Creator. Another reason is to experience the full potential of their existence beyond the material world. There are many other valid reasons for accepting Jesus Christ, as one's Lord and Savior; volumes of book could be written on that subject alone.

Verily, verily, I say unto you, except a corn of wheat fall into the ground and die, it abideth alone: but if it die, it bringeth forth much fruit. John 12:24

The process of dying to one's self, is sometimes glossed over or totally ignored by some evangelists and preachers, especially in our modern times. There is nothing wrong with loving one's self, we just have to love God more than we love ourselves; in addition we have to love others, as we love ourselves. Prior to accepting Jesus Christ as our savior, we establish certain patterns of behavior which we believe, are in our best interest to preserve our lives and further our best interest. There are certain activities we engage in, which relaxes us and diminishes the stress in our lives. We become accustomed to engaging in these activities. Ultimately these activities we choose to engage in may be beneficial or detrimental to us. These activities may also be moral or immoral, sinful or righteous. We also develop certain viewpoints and attitudes about the world, ourselves and others. Prior to accepting Jesus Christ, the way we live our lives are based on what we want; regardless, if what we want is good, evil, beneficial or detrimental to us.

When we accept Jesus Christ as our Lord and Savior we begin to change spiritually, emotionally and intellectually. The spiritual change is more subtle and less transparent than the emotional and intellectual changes. The spiritual change involves the work of the Holy Spirit. The emotional and intellectual changes can be immediate. The intellectual change is usually immediate, as we know we have chosen to make a change in our lives. We know on an intellectual level we will endeavor to be more loving and closer to God. We know intellectually that we are ultimately on our way to heaven and not hell. Emotionally, we are happy to be in a loving relationship with our Creator.

When I became a believer in Jesus Christ, I continued to sin. In fact my sin became worse, before it started to diminish in frequency and intensity. At age seven, I accepted Jesus Christ as my Lord and Savior. At age seven, I was not having sex with women I was not married to, I was not seeking revenge on my enemies, I was not going to strip clubs, and engaging in idolatrous behaviors. I don't believe I hated anyone at age seven. At age seven I was not intentionally associating with individuals who were bad influences on me. I'm sure I was committing some sins at age seven, but they were not the aforementioned listed sins.

From a moral perspective, I believe I became a more sinful person after I accepted Jesus Christ as my Lord and Savior. Again, this was primarily due to my age at accepting Jesus Christ, and also due to my free will choices. I accepted Jesus Christ as my Lord and Savior at the tender age of seven, as I grew and matured I had more opportunity to sin. I could have chosen not to hate. I could have chosen not to visit strip clubs. I could have chosen not to commit fornication, and I could have chosen not to engage in other sins; however, I chose to commit those sins. I can honestly state, that I regret committing those sins, because they gave birth to painful and tragic consequences in my life, and in the lives of others.

The Holy Sprit is helping me change my life; it is a painful process. Without this process being started, I'm confident I would have been killed early in life, and I would be currently burning in hell. Jesus Christ saved both my physical and spiritual life. The Holy Spirit is helping me become the absolute best version of Darnell Sherman; it is a process known as sanctification. I will never be perfect in this material world, but by the grace of God, I will progressively become more the man God wants me to be, until the day I leave this planet. Sanctification includes transforming my life, from reflecting my will and desires, to a life which reflects God's will and desires. I became tired of myself, so I died to myself spiritually and intellectually as much as I could; I am still in the process of doing so. I believe, I will continue to be in the process of dying to myself until I die physically, or until the Lord raptures me off this planet.

There is a freedom in surrendering one's free will to God, because we know God is good, loving, holy, and righteous. We lose ourselves; we are born again into the image and family of Jesus Christ. Again, spiritually we die to ourselves.

> *For I know the thoughts that I think toward you, saith the LORD, thoughts of peace, and not of evil, to give you an expected end. Jeremiah 29:11*

> *The thief cometh not, but for to steal, and to kill, and to destroy: I am come that they might have life, and that they might have it more abundantly. John 10:10*

If we hold on and trust God, there is an abundant life in Jesus Christ awaiting us in the next world. We simply have to keep our faith in Jesus Christ, and not give up, pray to him for help, and trust him with all of our hearts.

We may have an abundant life on earth in Jesus Christ, even in the midst of suffering and pain, and we may find meaning and purpose in the suffering and pain we face. Earthly pain and suffering is temporal.

That I may know him, and the power of his resurrection, and the fellowship of his suffering, being made conformable unto his death. Philippians 3:10

The abundant life in Jesus Christ may exist within us, even if we are penniless, sleeping in a cardboard box on the street, have no family or friends, in prison, or in excruciating pain.

As it is written, For thy sake we are killed all the day long; we are accounted as sheep for the slaughter. Nay, in all these things we are more than conquerors through him that loved us. Romans 8:36-37

Do not kill yourself, no matter what you are going through. God wants you alive and on earth at this moment in time. Find a meaning and a purpose in your suffering; Jesus Christ is there with you, the Holy Spirit is there with you, and your Heavenly Father is there with you. Pray to the Lord, and feel his presence in your life. God loves you.

Jesus Christ our Lord and Savior stated, the thief comes to steal, kill and to destroy. Do not allow the thief; the devil, to persuade you to destroy your life. God chose to create you, he did not have to create you, but he chose to create you, because he loves you dearly, and he loves you more than you know.

Mortal existence, mortal life is truly a gift from God. We don't have it forever; we have it for a short and temporary time upon the earth. Once it is gone, it is gone forever. After death, we will stand before God Almighty and be judged, and then we will be eternal spirits forever experiencing God's bliss, peace and love, or forever experiencing the pain of eternal condemnation in the fiery, horrors of hell. Value your mortality. Value your life on earth, because it is fleeting. Have a sense of urgency to become closer to God, and to follow his will for your life.

If you want to escape your pain and heartache do not commit suicide, you will most likely quadruple your pain and sorrow by committing suicide, and subsequently ending up in hell. I'm not suggesting that everyone whoever committed suicide is burning in hell, because it is possible that perhaps before they breathed their last breath, somehow, someway they repented of their sin and asked God to forgive them. I would not suggest that anyone take that chance. God will help you through your pain and sorrow. Jesus Christ stated, he left us the Holy Spirit which is the Comforter, who helps us through the hard times, and brings us in remembrance of all things.

Do not throw away the gift of life. Do not throw away the gift of your life. Touch the love, the intimate fellowship and peace you share with Jesus Christ. Feel and know that God's love exists within your heart, and there are rewards in heaven which await you, to be reveled in and enjoyed for all of eternity. You are not alone; the Lord's angels are all around you, protecting your heart and cheering you on.

Heavenly Father, I pray this prayer with tears in my eyes as you know; I am humbled and honored that you saw fit to create me. I am humbled and honored that you know me and communicate with me. I am humbled and honored that you love me Lord. Thank you for providing meaning and purpose in my life in so many majestic and powerful ways; the most important being my relationship with you Lord. Feeling and experiencing you in my life, is what carries me from day to day Lord. Feeling your love for me has made all the difference in my life Lord; it has literally stopped me from killing myself during dreadful moments of sorrow and depression... thank you Jesus! I pray Heavenly Father, for anyone reading this book; you know who he or she is Lord. I pray that you manifest your love to them in a very powerful way. I pray that you help them to realize they are loved beyond words by you Lord. Help them realize their life has a very important meaning and purpose, and that you are God, who changes night into day, water into wine, the sick into the whole, and the filthy into the righteous and clean. Put your angels of protection around the reader of these words Lord. For the readers of this book Lord, I ask that the Holy Spirit encourages them, and that you bless them, protect them, heal them, prosper them and keep them; in the mighty and precious name of our Lord and Savior; Jesus Christ, I pray, amen.

God is more powerful than your circumstances. God is more powerful than any human being, witch, sorcerer or devil. God is more powerful than any government, military or anything created. As a believer in Jesus Christ, the most powerful being in the universe loves you, eternally protects you and has your back through hard and good times.

But I will forewarn you whom ye shall fear: Fear him, which after he hath killed hath power to cast into hell; yea, I say unto you, Fear him. Luke 12:5

Are not two sparrows sold for a farthing? And one of them shall not fall on the ground without your Father. But the very hairs of your head are all numbered. Fear ye not therefore, ye are of more value than many sparrows. Luke 10:29-31

You are very important in this world, and you are very important to God. Time is expiring, and if you have accepted Jesus Christ as your Lord and Savior, you have nothing to fear, aside from a healthy fear and reverence for God, who loves you dearly and compassionately.

> *The fear of the LORD is the beginning of wisdom: a good understanding have all they that do his commandments: his praise endureth for ever. Palm 111:10*

The avoidance of human isolation and aloneness is a driving force in human motivation and behavior. The vast majority of humans strive for love, companionship and intimacy. The reality of the human condition is that we are alone in the empirical and material sense. We may be in a stadium of fifty-thousand people and experience a great sense of isolation and aloneness. We may wear the jersey or colors of a particular sports team, in order to further identify or join with others, who are also fans of the team we are cheering for. Yes, we want our team to win, but for those few hours of the game, we feel less isolated and alone, and we feel more connected to the other fans and to the overall experience. This is why it seems, at least from a fan's perspective sports is less about one's team winning or losing, and it is more about humans uniting, and acknowledging a common purpose, and cheering together for the success of a team. We unite to cheer and advocate for a common goal, in the hope of achieving a oneness or a deeper level of intimacy with each other.

> *I and my Father are one. ~ John 10:30*

> *And now I am no more in the world, but these are in the world, and I come to thee. Holy Father, keep through thine own name those whom thou hast given me, that they may be one, as we are. ~ John 17:11*

> *That they all may be one; as thou, Father, art in me, and I in thee, that they also may be one in us: that the world may believe that thou hast sent me. ~ John 17:21*

Jesus Christ addresses the issue of oneness; he states the Father and he are one. It seems this oneness has to do with the coalescing of the spirit of Jesus and the spirit of the Father, joining together to become one.

It seems some people kill themselves because they feel a great sense of isolation or aloneness. Perhaps they feel a lack of love in their lives. Jesus Christ can remedy the sense of being or feeling alone, isolated, and disconnected from the world, others and yourself. One may experience a sense of self-estrangement as well.

I want to acknowledge a distinction between being alone and isolated, and feeling alone and isolated. Humans are comprised of a spirit, soul and body. The human spirit is eternal and will live on forever, either in heaven or hell. The human spirit determines our nature, as it relates to good or evil. When humans are born, we are born with an evil spirit nature; our tendencies are to choose evil with abandon. This is why Jesus Christ stated, a human must be born again to enter into heaven.

> There was a man of the Pharisees, named Nicodemus, a ruler of the Jews: The same came to Jesus by night, and said unto him, Rabbi, we know that thou art a teacher come from God: for no man can do these miracles that thou doest, except God be with him. Jesus answered and said unto him, Verily, verily, I say unto thee, Except a man be born again, he cannot see the kingdom of God. Nicodemus saith unto him, How can a man be born when he is old? can he enter the second time into his mother's womb, and be born? Jesus answered, Verily, verily, I say unto thee, Except a man be born of water and of the Spirit, he cannot enter into the kingdom of God. That which is born of the flesh is flesh; and that which is born of the Spirit is spirit. Marvel not that I said unto thee, Ye must be born again. John 3:1-7

When one chooses to accept Jesus Christ as their Lord and Savior; one is essentially born again. The individual's nature changes from good to evil, in the sense the sanctification process begins. The sanctification process is simply the process of the individual, becoming more Christ like overtime. When one sins after being born again; not only are they sinning against God, they are also sinning against their own spiritual nature. The individual may seek forgiveness of God after sinning, and God is just and merciful to forgive.

An internal conflict emerges within the individual who accepts Jesus Christ, as their Lord and Savior. The individual is torn between good and evil; the individual can no longer gratuitously engage in sinful behaviors, without being convicted by the Holy Spirit and their own conscious.

As a single heterosexual male, I would love to have sex with beautiful women as much as possible; however, I choose not to…why; primarily, because it would be a sin before God, and I would reap the consequences from God for violating his law. I would also know that I am sinning, while committing the act, which would diminish the overall pleasure of the act. Overall, this is a good deterrent to fornication, because there are dangerous consequences of leading a sexually promiscuous life. Some of the consequences could be contracting and spreading sexually transmitted diseases, unwanted pregnancies, abortions, adultery, sexual exploitation, sex trafficking, prostitution, and a whole host of other harmful and deadly consequences; avoid this trap.

There are negative spiritual consequences for committing sin, and there are negative consequences in the material world for committing sin. The best scenario is to be born again through Jesus Christ and not sin, yet while in this material world we will never be perfect, but daily we can become closer to the individual God wants us to be.

Sin could range from lusting in our hearts, to murdering people randomly; which seems to be an epidemic in this era. The sin could range from a prideful heart, and believing we are more righteous or superior to others, to robbing a bank. The reality is Christian or not, we all sin. The key is to be born again, seek forgiveness and ask God to help us overcome the sin we struggle with. Experiencing shame and guilt after we sin is a good thing, because it is a deterrent for sinning in the future. Most people don't want to experience shame or guilt. Even while experiencing shame and guilt, we may repent and ask God to forgive us of our sins, and God will forgive us. We need to know that God has forgiven us, after we seek repentance, and then we need to forgive ourselves and assess how we can avoid sinning in the future, and ask God to help us not to sin moving forward. Jesus Christ was the only human whoever walked the earth, and never committed a sin. Don't judge yourself and others so harshly, because we are all sinners; that being said, try not to sin. The only way we can begin to sin less is through the power of the Holy Spirit. I am a witness, regrettably I still sin, but through the power of the Holy Spirit, I don't sin as much as I used to, and for that I thank God. This is not a competition; perhaps, I am not the human being who is closest to God, but I thank God that I am closer to God, than I was a year ago. Hallelujah…thank you Jesus!

The goal is to reduce the frequency and intensity of our sin, and to become more like Jesus Christ on a daily basis. We will be perfect in heaven; however, we have to endeavor to endure and overcome temptation while on the earth.

> *And he that taketh not his cross, and followeth after me, is not worthy of me. Matthew 10:38*

> *But he that shall endure unto the end, the same shall be saved. Matthew 24:13*

> *Enter ye in at the strait gate: for wide is the gate, and broad is the way, that leadeth to destruction, and many there be which go in thereat: Because strait is the gate, and narrow is the way, which leadeth unto life, and few there be that find it. Matthew 7:13-14*

The soul of a human is comprised of the intellect and personality. Obviously, this is a very important aspect of the individual's being. Whoever you are, God created you with the wonderful personality you have. God created you with the gifts you have, to touch the lives of others in a positive way. God wants you to be a vessel for his use and purposes; this will bring meaning and purpose to one's existence. God can help your personality and intellect to be all it can be, to be exceptional beyond your imagination. You don't lose yourself by being born again, you are born again into everything you have the potential of being, within the uniqueness of you, and in the heart of Jesus Christ. We can only reach the full potential of ourselves, through being born again in Jesus Christ. The only way to be truly liberated and free is through Jesus Christ. We are no longer enslaved to culture, to money, to sex, to emotion, to the opinions of others or to social status. We are truly free in Jesus Christ.

Logic and reason has their place, but as believers in Jesus Christ, we walk by faith and not by sight. We have to abandon our own theories of the way the world works, and the way things should be, to adopt God's perspective on the world and life, the best we can. When I was younger, I wanted to fight for justice. Being a young Black male in America, I experienced painful racism which hurt me. I could have joined a street gang and sought revenge and justice through violence and crime. I could have joined the Communist party and advocated revolution; I considered those possibilities as viable options in my life; however, I never chose them. I chose to follow the teachings of Jesus Christ, to love my enemies, to bless those who curse me, and pray for those who despitefully use me. I am not perfect, and it is hard for me to love my enemies, to bless those who curse me, and to pray for those who despitefully use me; however, with the help of the Holy Spirit, I try to do these things; not really because I want to, but because God wants me to. It is less stressful to forgive, than to hold a grudge and seek revenge.

God has blessed me with certain wisdom and knowledge, for which I am grateful. As Christians, we have to accept God's philosophy of life, which will only enhance our own intellect and understanding of life, both in the material and spiritual world. God opened up the Red Sea to help, Moses and the children of Israel escape the army of Egypt. What of this? If God opened up the Red Sea, created the universe; what choice do we have but to adopt his ways, his philosophy and to serve him with the gift of life, which he has visited upon all of us.

HERE AND NOW

Take therefore no thought for the morrow: for the morrow shall take thought for the things of itself. Sufficient unto the day is the evil thereof. Matthew 6:34

Looking unto Jesus the author and finisher of our faith; who for the joy that was set before him endured the cross, despising the shame, and is set down at the right hand of the throne of God. Hebrews 12:2

If it was not for salvation through Jesus Christ, I would either be dead or in an insane asylum. Spending my days worrying about the future, would be a very easy task for me. I don't know the future, and there are many threats and dangers in the world; therefore, worrying about the future would be a very easy task to engage in.

I often asked myself, should I live in the here and now, or focus more on the past or future, or focus on another place; where I am not? In some ways, it is a question which is not really valid, because no matter what; I am in the here and now, and I cannot escape it, despite where my mental focus may be. I have decided to have my mental focus in the here and now; I am not always successful at this task; however, it is something I endeavor to do.

When I am more focused on the here (present time) and now (present location), I experience more of what the present moment and location has to offer. The experience of the here and now is more enhanced, when I embrace and am focused on it. At times focusing on the here and now may be a pleasant or unpleasant experience. I find that I worry less when I focus on the here and now, because it brings into focus the immediacy of my experience, my strengths, my vulnerabilities and my need for God. Focusing on the here and now also enhances my relationships. When I am communicating with another, I am psychologically present for them, and experiencing the uniqueness of the interaction, while understanding it could be the last time I interact with them; therefore, I value and enjoy the moment more.

On occasions in the past, I've had conversations with people who were not psychologically present with me. I admit; I have done this too, but it is best practice to be psychologically present when communicating in person.

As a believer in Jesus Christ, much of my general focus is on my eternal future in heaven. This motivates me and essentially guides my behavior in the here and now. My relationship with Jesus Christ provides my life with purpose and meaning in the here and now. The eternal

DARNELL L. SHERMAN MS AMFT

warmth of God's love, protection and peace awaits me in heaven, because I have accepted Jesus Christ as my Lord and Savior.

My enduring overall focus is not the here and now, it is on a place and time I've never experienced before; it is on my future in heaven. My immediate focus is on the here and now on earth; a healthy dichotomy, which assists me in successfully navigating the opera of this material world.

When I am in pain or experiencing trauma, I focus on my eternity in heaven, realizing that the current pain and trauma is temporal and will not last forever. I also pray and ask God to remove my pain and trauma, and help me to find some meaning, purpose or lesson in it. In times of extreme pain or sorrow, I close my eyes and cry out to God for help; through prayer I intently seek God's mercy, grace and wisdom. I have found this strategy to be of a great help and comfort. After the wave of pain and trauma has passed, I attempt to find some meaning or purpose in it, always in consultation with the Lord. *"Heavenly Father, what am I supposed to learn from this?"*

The pain of existence is difficult to cope with successfully. We can't simply exist like a rock on a beach; we have to do things to maintain our existence physically. We have to eat and drink, eliminate waste, be clothed and sheltered from the elements and the dangers of life. We have to interact with others, maintain our sanity and discover a purpose for our existence. I don't believe any of us asked to come into existence; nevertheless, we are all here, and we have to find a meaning for our existence. We are blessed to exist; God chose to create each and every one of us out of love. The ultimate purpose for everyone's existence is to know God, and to have a loving relationship with him, through his only begotten son, Jesus Christ; a simple, but true answer. This ultimate purpose provides more immediate purposes for our existence, such as praying, developing an intimate relationship with the Lord, reading the Holy Bible, attending church, helping others and telling others about Jesus Christ. We are also told by God to love him, ourselves and others, and to forgive those who have harmed us. One's life is flooded with meaning and purpose, as a result of accepting Jesus Christ as one's Lord and Savior. We have to see the meaning and purpose which exists, and grab hold onto it, and never let go. We must seek to live it out and fulfill the purpose God has for our lives. We try to become more Christ like everyday, and the uniqueness of who we really are begins to shine through.

An existence in hell is the only pain and trauma which lasts forever. The pain and trauma which exists in this material world is temporal; whatever it is, it will not last forever. For born again Christians pain and trauma ends when we leave this world; no more pain, trauma or heartache will exist after we die or experience the rapture. For those who do not believe in Jesus Christ, death is just the beginning of their pain, trauma, and torment, and it will never end.

Accept Jesus Christ as your Lord and Savior. You can do this by sincerely praying this prayer:

"Heavenly Father, I ask that you forgive me of my sins, and I accept your son, Jesus Christ as my Lord and Savior. I place my trust and life in his hands. Thank you for saving me. In the name of Jesus Christ I pray, amen."

THE ERRONEOUS JOY OF NOTHINGNESS

Just to exist. Just to be. Not to try. Not to move. To die of thirst. To die of starvation. Pretending to be a big white boulder submerged in the sea off the shore of Dana Point. Yet, I'm breathing; the boulder is not. I have free will; the boulder does not. I am betraying nothingness to meet the minimal needs of human life, food and shelter? What does the man sleeping on the bus bench, and eating from garbage cans know, that I don't? What did my mother know that I do not? A sixth grade education, she never learned to drive a car, a Black woman living in a violent and racist world, with very limited financial resources, successfully raised five children. Thank you Sedalia. Thank you mother. Nothingness knocked on her door; however, she never let it in, she vigorously eluded it.

To do nothing. To expect nothing. To have no consequences. To have no free will. Yet, to embrace nothingness is a free will choice. Humanity is saddled with free will, and the act of choosing whatever is something, and not nothing. True nothingness, pure nothingness does not exist; therefore, we may not embrace it. By the simple act of choosing nothingness, we destroy it in our lives. Perhaps it has to sneak upon us unawares; yet to allow that to occur is also a free will choice.

> *And he said unto them, Go ye into all the world, and preach the gospel to every creature. He that believeth and is baptized shall be saved; but he that believeth not shall be damned. And these signs shall follow them that believe; In my name shall they cast out devils; they shall speak with new tongues; They shall take up serpents; and if they drink any deadly thing, it shall not hurt them; they shall lay hands on the sick, and they shall recover. Mark 15:18*

> *Then said Jesus unto his disciples, If any man will come after me, let him deny himself, and take up his cross, and follow me. Mark 16:24*

> *And he called his ten servants, and delivered them ten pounds, and said unto them, Occupy till I come. Luke 19:13*

God does not want us to embrace the illusion of nothingness. We do not exist in the world alone. God has specific things he wants his children to do. As much as I would like to sit on a jetty all day, every day and stare into the Pacific Ocean, and simply write poetry for the rest of my life. I choose not to do that, for a number of reasons. Number one, I don't believe it is God's will for my life. Number two, it would not be safe. Number three, I would not be able to generate a sufficient income to purchase the physical necessities of life. This is not to say, that I cannot indulge in such an activity at times; however, I have chosen not to make it a primary purpose of my life. I want to fulfill God's purpose for my life, and it is not sitting on a jetty everyday writing poetry.

I would like to escape the violence, immorality and decay of this world, and simply view and embrace the world's beauty, majesty and splendor; however, it is not healthy to live in denial, nor is it healthy to deny my contribution to the deplorable state of the world by the sins I have committed, or by my passivity. I am not above it all; however, it is a prideful temptation for me, to believe that I am. It is a prideful temptation, to believe if everyone was like me, the condition of the world would be so much better. Literally, if everyone was like me, I believe the world would be more paganistic and idolatrous. It is only by the unmerited grace of God, that I am not a hedonistic pagan indulging in sexual abandon and vengeance. I can admit that, because it is true. I am not a good person, the only good which exists within me, is because of Jesus Christ and the Holy Spirit. I have to deny my ungodly desires, because if I do not they will eventually lead to my destruction, and ultimately to my eternal condemnation.

I believe in Jesus Christ as my Lord and Savior. I choose to follow the guidance of the Holy Spirit the majority of the time. The guidance of the Holy Spirit leads me to a holy, righteous, meaningful and loving existence. I war against myself, the world and the enemy. It appears the things that I love and find beautiful in this world, does me the most harm, because my defenses are down.

Suicide is an act of free will choice. It is not diving into a sea of nothingness, or into a sea of non-existence; total annihilation of one's spirit, soul and body; this does not exist. Suicide is a rejection of life, and a violation of the law of God. We will all have to kneel before God, and give an account of our lives. When God asks one, *"Why did you kill yourself, why did you fail to turn to me for help"?* What will the person say? Suicide is jumping from the frying pan, literally into the fire. When humans die, they either live in heaven or hell forever, depending on their free will choices upon the earth. With freedom of choice comes responsibility. We live in an era, where many cry for the freedom to do whatever they want; however, few embrace the responsibility which comes with the freedom. There are consequences to our choices; make your choices good ones and seek God for guidance.

We are not simply individuals on this planet all alone; God exists, angels exist, and evil spirits exist. To believe we just exist, and we are not being tempted and influenced by spiritual forces, is a critical error in judgment.

The thief cometh not, but for to steal, and to kill, and to destroy: I am come that they might have life, and that they might have it more abundantly. John 10:10

Human immunity from our spiritual enemy is only found in Jesus Christ. God can protect us and shield us from our enemy.

Ye are of God, little children, and have overcome them: because greater is he that is in you, than he that is in the world. I John 4:4

My meaning in life comes from having a loving, educational and fulfilling relationship with my Lord and Savior; Jesus Christ. It also comes from attempting to fulfill his will for my life, which includes loving God, loving myself, loving others, trying to help others, praying for others, and sharing the Gospel of Christ with others. I have prayed for whoever read these words, that God will bless and protect you, and that your eyes and heart, may be open to the truth and love of Jesus Christ, if they are not already open to it. Much love and peace to you!

OPERA OF EXISTENCE

I am crucified with Christ: nevertheless I live; yet not I, but Christ liveth in me: and the life which I now live in the flesh I live by the faith of the Son of God, who loved me, and gave himself for me. Galatians 2:20

He that findeth his life shall lose it: and he that loseth his life for my sake shall find it. Matthew 10:39

My authenticity is born again, better, holier, purer and more beautiful than it ever was, because of the blood of Jesus Christ, and its transformative power.

Losing my authenticity…losing my wants and desires…not doing what I want…not getting what I want…losing my self…alienating me from my self, in order to take on the image, values, will and desire of my Lord and Savior, Jesus Christ. I am born again strong in the image of Jesus Christ; struggling to become more like him on a daily basis. Finding and integrating myself in my Creator.

Subduing my will…to perform the will of Christ, which may be directly opposed to my will. God visited free will upon me…I choose to follow the will of Christ, rather to follow my will, except when the will of Christ and my will are aligned. My will is becoming God's will for my life; becoming, evolving into what will eventually be perfection in heaven. Moving closer towards perfection on a daily basis.

I become all I can be, my personality, my uniqueness, my beauty, my life is infinitely enhanced and maximized through being born again in the blood of Jesus Christ. I am losing the worst parts of my being, and growing the best parts of my being through the love and guidance of the Holy Spirit. My will becoming God's will for my life. Thank you Jesus!

COVID-19 PANDEMIC

Poetry? Ancient prophecies being fulfilled. Before our eyes. In a matter of hours our lives changed. What is next? Technology social media humans more isolated and distant than ever. IBM AT&T Verizon Apple Samsung Amazon Microsoft bringing the world closer? College and restaurants where are the conversations? Where is the human interaction? Four people at a table. Each staring at a cell phone. Deconstructing human conversation. Filtering words, through emotionless machines. Losing intimacy. Losing intimacy. Alcohol, opiates, LSD and marijuana numbing a nation to reality. Digital screen zombies. Programmed to want what is not required.

Bel Biv Devoe, sang I thought it was me. *"I thought it was me who makes the girl this way, I came to find out she's like that everyday. I thought it was me that makes that girl so wild, I found out she's like that with all the guys."* B.B.D. (I Thought It Was Me)? (1989) MCA Records. Wake up call. Romance beyond the material is the best way to go. Romance beyond sex is the best way to go. Love, true intimacy, understanding, trust, romance beyond this world and marriage before sex; the best way...the best way to go. The way of God is always the best.

Social distancing. Emotional distancing. Spiritual distancing. Wear a mask and stay sick feet apart, sick feet apart? Six feet apart. Our machines and technology became our new lovers. Cell phones, lap tops desk tops watch out for the new virus. Spiritual and psychological addictions to machines.

Until the Covid-19 Pandemic never did I understand how gullible. How gullible many people can become. I fail to understand how people can reject Jesus Christ as Lord and Savior. I think, I believe, I am beginning to understand how many people will accept the mark of the beast. The hand or forehead; just a small undetectable chip; it takes less than five seconds to implant. Distribution sites Dodger Stadium, Angel Stadium and various hospitals near you. Hollywood celebrities creating songs for commercials urging, urging pushing, pushing citizens to receive the new form of evil worship into their bodies. No need to carry money, identification, driver's licenses, medical insurance cards, social security cards, credit cards or cards of any type; no more checks; it's all in the chip...so convenient; no need for concern of identity theft; just sell your immortal soul to the antichrist; no forgiveness after receiving the mark; a one way trip to hell it is.

We took the Covid-19 vaccine. I took the Covid-19 vaccine. The Covid-19 vaccine is not the mark of the beast. I think, I believe, the distribution of the Covid-19 vaccine is a dry run for the distribution of the mark of the beast. I asked God *"Should I take the Covid-19 vaccine?"* I believe he told me yes. I trust God for my protection, yet I take vaccines and have access to human weapons. My greatest weapons is the *"Sword of the Spirit (Ephesians 6:17)"*. I am not a medical doctor. I have not earned a medical degree; nevertheless, my advice is this; never allow anyone to implant a chip into or on your body. My advice is this, never allow anyone to place a mark on your body, especially your hand or forehead, and especially if the mark has any connection to the number 666. Jesus Christ is Lord. Serve Jesus Christ. Trust Jesus Christ. Love Jesus Christ. Give your life to Jesus Christ. The best advice I have.

LAGUNA BEACH

He was killed
Because
He was not wearing a seat belt

Will you make a decision
Without
Your cell phone or computer?

What of the spiritual
Undertones
Overtones
Sidetones

We simply accept
Least controversial
Least holy
Most dangerous

Beyond
A physiological organ
What of the human heart?

Beyond
A fanatical hypothesis
What of the eternal human spirit?

Beyond the U.S. Constitution
Flaws of human law
What of everlasting justice?

To rap
Playing basketball
Dunking and fronting

Brittany wearing a yellow polka dot bikini
Wayfarers on
Sipping vanilla coke

As the world comes to an end
Ushered in…is God's judgment
Who shall be able to stand?

I DON'T LIKE SUSHI

I am me

Her life is dynamic

Pretend enthusiasm

Is not my thing

She loves her new lipstick

She sings

"I'm visiting Buenos Aires"

"two weeks, I can't wait".

Sitting on the jetty thinking

She asks

"Is this all you want to do?"

I ask

"What am I doing?"

Staring into the Pacific again

She says

"Let's go buy sushi for dinner"

I say

"I don't like sushi"

She wants more

I want less

SATURN 17

We live
We die

What is in-between
What really lasts...

Beyond this mortality

Endeavoring to realize
Endeavoring to discover
Endeavoring to experience

True love
True meaning
To touch our Creator
Before we die

NM

Running away from who we are

Looking away from our reflection

So familiar with ourselves

We no longer stand it…making us sick

Where is the escape from the here?

Where is the escape from the now?

No matter how rich or how poor

No matter how many vacations

No matter how many new lovers

No matter how many new drugs

No matter how much money

No matter new experiences

No need to sell your soul

No need to kill your self

We cannot truly escape ourselves

We cannot truly lose ourselves

Until we find ourselves in Jesus Christ

WORLD WITHOUT END (PART III)

My eyes gazed upon her
Her looks seduced me
Wanting to rescue her

Wanting to pull her...
Out of her world
Into my world

Entering her world
Touching her
Estrangement and uneasiness
Enveloped me
Toxicity affected me

Trying to convince her to leave
She laughed, smiled and kept dancing
Beckoning me...holding her
A passionless and empty kiss
Maybe love could grow?

Baby, please leave this...
Material and temporal world of misery
She continued dancing and smiling
I could not stay...wanting to destroy her world
Leaving her world

Returning...returning
To Truth
Returning...returning
To my first love

Returning to Christ

DARNELL L. SHERMAN MS AMFT

VIOLENCE OF EXISTENCE

Jesus Christ

I have no right to make demands of you
I am like an ant
I am less than ant in your presence

Jesus Christ
You created me
My existence would not be without you

You give my life purpose
You give my life meaning
You give my life significance

Delusional me to pretend
Purpose, meaning and significance without you

Only you Lord
Ignites true meaning…true love…true life

Only you Lord
Rescues from nothingness…from despair…from eternal condemnation

80's HEAVEN

Maybe when I die?

Maybe when the rapture?

God will allow me to travel time?

Live in the 80's again?

With the music

With the fashion

With the fun

With the youth

Without the mistakes

Without the sin

TRUE PSYCHOTHERAPY

Between morning and afternoon
Middle of June

Betrayal and beating
This world is fleeting

Wanting to die
Believing a lie

Holy Spirit spoke
For me not to choke

Big picture He showed
My depression slowed

Death comes no matter
Heed not evil chatter

My life's meaning addressed
Holy Spirit expressed

Christ a man of sorrows and acquainted with grief
Realization a relief which spurred my belief

God uttered, you I shall love and bless
My expectations of humans became less

Began my life of estrangement from counterfeit love
Embracing a greater love from above

I learned, to my life only Christ holds the clock
As I stand upon the only solid rock

OBLIGATION

Contemplating

Being quiet…being still

Motionless…simply thinking

Simply being

My preferred state

Future noble actions

Future actions of necessity

Being quiet…being still

Motionless…simply thinking

Simply being

Simply dreading… disturbing

The here…the now

With movement…with effort

Noble and necessary tasks await

What of responsibility

What of life

Prefer to pray all day

Simply being in God's presence

So peaceful…so significant

Yet…the burden of human existence

I move

WRAPPED IN TIME

We dress fashionably
Yet no hope inside

We have whitened teeth
Yet no hope inside

We have the newest smart phones
Yet no hope inside

We have the newest automobiles
Yet no hope inside

We have fans and followers
Yet no hope inside

We live in Beverly Hills
Yet no hope inside

We live in the Hamptons
Yet no hope inside

We live in South Beach
Yet no hope inside

We live in Newport Beach
Yet no hope inside

We sleep on the street
Yet no hope inside

We are addicted to drugs and alcohol
Yet no hope inside

We are addicted to sex
Yet no hope inside

We are addicted to pornography
Yet no hope inside

We play video games
Yet no hope inside

We are religious
Yet no hope inside

We are married with children
Yet no hope inside

We are heterosexual
Yet no hope inside

We are homosexual
Yet no hope inside

We are transgender
Yet no hope inside

We are in a gang
Yet no hope inside

We are atheists
Yet no hope inside

We are republicans
Yet no hope inside

We are democrats
Yet no hope inside

We are human
Yet no hope inside

Activity expiring our lives
Time evaporates

We have cultural and familial validation
We kept up appearances

Then what?
Jesus Christ our only hope

BARBARISM 401

They rebel for freedom

Having their causes

Enlightened and progressive

They paint themselves

In the finest traditions of tyrants

They are unaware

Of change within themselves

No tolerance for dissenting views

Annihilation of the enemy

Censoring all opinions

Except their own

The worst outcome

Hate seizes control

Tolerance a distant memory

Book burnings

No love for the precious life

Inside growing

DARNELL L. SHERMAN MS AMFT

Who never takes a breath

Sliced from their mother and vacuumed out

Murdering the most vulnerable

Personal responsibility and free will

Thrown in the river of denial

Self made savages

Civilized and sophisticated

They paint themselves

PRESS CONFERENCE

Clepto: I appreciate all of you coming. Perhaps, this is an extension of my baptism; a public recognition of my being born again through the blood of Jesus Christ. I am a Christian, and I am not perfect. I am a sinner, saved by the grace of God. I make this a public declaration today. Now, I will take a few questions:

Reporter 1:   Are you a homosexual or a bisexual?

Clepto: No, I am neither. I am a heterosexual.

Reporter 1:   So you are attracted to biological females?

Clepto: Yes.

Reporter 2:   So, you are over fifty years old, and have no children and have never been married?

Clepto: That is correct.

Reporter 2:   Why is that the case?

Clepto: Several women have not accepted my marriage proposals. Per the Holy Bible, I believe that a man and a woman should be married prior to choosing to have a child or children.

Reporter 3:   So you're indicating you have proposed marriage to several women?

Clepto: That is correct.

Reporter 3:   Who are these women?

Clepto: I'm not going into specifics regarding this.

Reporter 4:   Are you a virgin?

Clepto: No, I am not; however, I should be. I have committed fornication in my life with women, and I have asked God to forgive me for those sins.

Reporter 4:   So you had sexual intercourse with a woman or women?

Clepto: That is correct; again, those were sinful acts I have repented of. I have to repent of sin on a daily basis.

Reporter 4:   What kind of sin?

Clepto: Again, I'm not going into specifics in this area; however, I will say the frequency and intensity of my sin has diminished over the years, through the process of sanctification, and most of all through the power of the Holy Spirit.

Reporter 4:   Why do you consider sex between a man and a woman a sinful act?

      DARNELL L. SHERMAN MS AMFT

Clepto:	The law of God states, that a man and a woman are only allowed to have sex if they are married to each other, and all other forms of sex is sin.
Reporter 4:	Do you agree with the law?
Clepto:	I do.
Reporter 4:	Why do you agree with it?
Clepto:	Simply, because it is God's law and he knows best, and there are negative consequences for violating God's law.
Reporter 1:	What are the negative consequences?
Clepto:	Well, they could be numerous and varied; however, a few of the consequences could be an unwanted pregnancy, abortion, sexually transmitted diseases, exploitation, emotional turmoil, adultery and eternal condemnation.
Reporter 2:	Do you want to get married?
Clepto:	Yes; I would love to be married, if it is God's will for my life, and I meet a woman who I am spiritually and emotionally compatible with, and she is willing to marry me. Women have free will. I cannot force a woman to marry me.
Reporter 3:	Do you believe you are a good candidate for marriage?
Clepto:	That is not for me to determine; however, I am trying hard to be the man God wants me to be. One more question.
Reporter 4:	Are you lonely?
Clepto:	No.
Reporter 4:	Just a quick follow up, why are you not lonely?
Clepto:	The Holy Spirit lives within my heart, and Jesus Christ has promised to never leave me or forsake me. Thank you all for coming.
Reporter 2:	Just one more question?
Clepto:	Again, thank you and may our only Lord and Savior, Jesus Christ bless you all.

REBEL HEART

A discovery

The world cannot
The world does not give me
What I want

The world only teases
The world never satisfies

Like a self deluded alcoholic
Believing the next drink will satisfy
Chasing until death

The world advertises true fulfillment
The world advertises true purpose
Overrated sex
Overrated money
Overrated power

Surrendering to truth
Surrendering to...
The death of my vanity

I am a true rebel
Rebelling against me
Rebelling against the world
Rebelling against the enemy

Joining the Army of Jesus Christ

PASSION (PART II)

My passion for vengeance
My passion for lust
My passion for power
My passion for pride
My passion for vanity
My passion for money
My passion for life

Deliver me Lord

Discipline

Ultimately

Only my passion for Jesus Christ should be unrestrained

Heavenly Father

Regardless of all

Help me to submit my will to you

I remember June

I will miss June in September

Thank you Holy Spirit!

TIN FOIL RING

A million dollars

Wrapped around a finger

They don't understand me

They like me

Understanding does not exist

I can leave it all beyond

Except one

One relationship

One dynamic

One difference

One life

One true love

DANIELLE

She's down to earth

Loves steaks and green beans

Mashed potatoes and brown gravy

She wears leather

Speaks gently

Engaging and peaceful

Danielle a woman of grace

God visited majestic beauty upon her

Wisdom and knowledge grace her

Man and woman becoming one

Holy matrimony

TORRENTIAL

Of the downpour

Of the deluge

Of the cascade

Of the rainstorm

Do you remember…

Do you remember?

That one special raindrop

That one unique raindrop

Landing on your flesh

Different from all the others

Guided from the heavens

Falling thousands of feet

Through time and space

With a single mission

Of touching you

> *Sing unto the Lord with Thanksgiving; sing praise upon the harp unto our God: Who covereth the heaven with clouds, who prepareth rain for the earth, who maketh grass to grow upon the mountains. Psalm 147:7-8*

DARNELL L. SHERMAN MS AMFT

LUPE

She waned
She appeared perfect

Pretty eyes
Bright smile

Woman
God's most beautiful
Creation

Gentle and soft
Caring and lovely

She helped me
Her presence
I was grateful
She epitomizes beauty

STRIVE

We live on this rock…
Rotating and floating in space
We come and go on this planet

The Word of God
Is like fresh air
As we are under water drowning

Gasping for air…
Rushing to the surface
For a life saving breath

DARNELL L. SHERMAN MS AMFT

SPRAY PAINTING APPLES

For us the pain will not last
Forgotten anguish of the past

While we're still wet from the storms
The love of Christ warms

Our abundance of tears
Our loneliness disappears

Graciously touching the sublime
Betraying our mistress of time

Hang in there
Never despair

Our perfect meaningful endeavor
Trusting God forever

Becoming less…not more
We increase the score

IN TIME

Wrapped in flesh

We exist

Like a tiger in a cage

Christ is our escape

We are spirits in the material world

We are spirits wrapped in flesh

Christ transcends our flesh

Christ transcends our cage

Our only true freedom

Our only true freedom

TRIGGER FINGER

M-16 A2

AK-47

Mossberg 940 Semi-Auto

Remington 44. Magnum

Why do I want to squeeze?

In the world

Make things right?

Express feelings of rage?

Revenge?

Nay, despite the feeling

Nay, despite the reason

Nay, despite the thoughts

Love God

Love yourself

Love others

Value God's commandments

Thou shalt not kill

Value human love

Value human life

Value God's love

Obey God's commandments

HUMAN BEINGS ON EARTH

We dance

We sing

We run

We hide

Yet we are vulnerable

Truly cannot protect ourselves

We are eternal spirits

Wrapped in flesh

In the material world

Only safety is in Jesus Christ

A semi-auto shotty

Loaded and cocked

Illusion of safety

Better than nothing?

Nevertheless,

Not comparable to the safety

We have in Jesus Christ

Thank you Holy Spirit!

DARNELL L. SHERMAN MS AMFT

DUST IN MY EYES

Man from dust
Woman from flesh

In marriage
Man and woman
Sex is a blessing

Outside of marriage
Sex is a curse
Lust never fulfilled
Competition never won

There is no satiation
Fornication
Opera of death

A vision more lovely than woman
I've not known
Yet there is a devil

Who uses
Who employs
Who tempts

A world beyond flesh
A world beyond material
A life beyond mortality

Temporal sensations
Not the answer
Temporal pleasures
Not the answer

King David knew
From Eve to Jezebel
They are here
I am here

Her hand in marriage
Love beyond the temporal
Love beyond this world
Two shall become one in Christ
The only way

EXISTENTIAL RESOLUTION

Mortal life

Is the dream

We are living the dream

We awake to reality

Of our choices

To eternal life and love

Or

To eternal life and pain

Universe

Of where did you come

What is the origin of existence?

We were not always here

This was not always here

Who brought time into existence?

Trapped in time

Trapped in mortality

Our freedom

Only way of true escape

Not in death…

Only in Jesus Christ

Life and love…without end

TRUE ULTIMATE FIGHTER

Power lies not in the gun

Power lies not in the gang

Power lies not in numbers

Power lies not in muscles

Power lies not in intellect

Power lies not in money

Power lies not in beauty

Power lies not in chains and knives

Power resides only in God

He distributes it as he will

Ultimate power resides in God

Follow God's will

> *And Jesus came and spake unto them, saying, all power is given unto me in heaven and in earth. Matthew 28:18*

THE WAY WE ARE

We condemn the whore
We make jokes about her
She spreads disease
She violates the law
She is an evil sinner
We would never kiss her
We will never have sex with her

The pretty church girl
We try to get next to
We spend our time and money
To convince her we are worthy
We want to kiss her
We want to have sex with her
We want to infect her with our lust and sin

Our hypocrisy
Our fornication
Our sin
The way we are

We're the horniest boys
With corniest ploys
We take the easiest girls
To our sleaziest worlds...
All that we live for, you'll regret
All you remember, we'll forget

Depeche Mode; The Dead of Night (2001) Mute Records

THIS IS NOT LOVE

Treachery mixed with emotional cruelty
Our lives of vanity…
Our lives of vanity
Makes me vomit

This is not love
Whatever else it may be…
It is not love

Evil is often the things we do
Evil is often the things we say

Lives of sin and delusion
Babe…I'm no longer willing to trade heaven
For a perversion of love

Staring into the waves of the Pacific
With you in my arms girl
Hopeless prayers with no repentance

Always waiting for the wrath
You always denied
Girl…it is just a matter of time

GO AND SIN NO MORE

There is a movement in the Christian community, which erroneously suggests, that all an individual has to do is to simply accept Jesus Christ as their Lord and Savior, and once that is done; they may blatantly sin without any negative consequences at all from the Lord. The proponents of this dangerous perspective, also suggests that when a Christian sins, the Christian should not feel a sense of guilt or remorse over their sin.

An inhibition against feelings of guilt or remorse over committing evil acts, is a symptom of an Anti-Social Personality Disorder, which characterizes the behaviors of sociopaths.

If a Christian murders a person in cold blood, the Christian should feel guilty about the evil act of murder they committed, and in addition they should experience a sense of remorse over it. Failure to do so, would not be Christ like, and would suggest that the Christian may be a sociopath.

One of God's commandments is *"Thou shalt not kill. Exodus 20:13"*. God also gave Moses nine other commandments. Some members of the Christian community will label other Christians, who adhere to the law of God and attempt to keep it; legalistic and wrong in their approach to God's law. I beg to differ; there is nothing wrong with adhering to the law of God, and attempting to keep it. In fact, we are told in numerous passages of the Holy Bible we are to acknowledge and keep God's law. The high rates of crime, violence, abortion, broken families, suicide and drug addiction in America, can be traced to violations of God's law.

Let us hear the conclusion of the whole matter: Fear God, and keep his commandments: for this is the whole duty of man. For God shall bring every work into judgment, with every secret thing, whether it be good, or whether it be evil. Ecclesiastes 12:14

Think not that I am come to destroy the law, or the prophets: I am not come to destroy, but to fulfil. Matthew 5:17

What shall we say then? Shall we continue in sin, that grace may abound? God forbid. How shall we, that are dead to sin, live any longer therein? Know ye not, that so many of us as were baptized into Jesus Christ were baptized into his death? Therefore we are buried with him by baptism into death: that like as Christ was raised up from the dead by the glory of the Father, even so we also should walk in newness of life. Romans 6:1-4

And when he had called the people unto him with his disciples also, he said unto them, Whosoever will come after me, let him deny himself, and take up his cross, and follow me. For whosoever will save his life shall lose it; but whosoever shall lose his life for my sake and the gospel's, the same shall save it. Mark 8:34-35

Christians are saved by the grace of God, and we cannot earn our salvation, because we have all sinned, and deserve to be in hell. Jesus Christ made a way for us to escape the flames of hell, as a result of loving us dearly, being crucified on the cross, and being resurrected three days later.

We receive eternal salvation by believing in Jesus Christ, and accepting him as our Lord and Savior. Once we are saved, we are born again; our evil nature has been transformed into good. This is where a conflict begins between our flesh, and the Holy Spirit who comes to reside within us when we are saved. I used to enjoy going to strip clubs and watching naked women dance. I enjoyed talking to naked, beautiful women I never met before. Yet, I knew this was wrong, and I was convicted of the Holy Spirit of this sin. Despite this knowledge and conviction and feelings of guilt and remorse, I kept going to strip clubs, until the consequences of this sin started manifesting itself in the material world, and then I stopped, by the grace of God.

My son, despise not the chastening of the LORD; neither be weary of his correction: For whom the LORD loveth he correcteth; even as a father the son in whom he delighteth. Proverbs 3:11-12

I believe it's been over twenty years since I stepped foot in a strip club, and it was the Holy Spirit who empowered me to overcome this sin. As a believer in Jesus Christ, I retained my free will to either attend strip clubs or not. I could have chosen to keep attending strip clubs; however, the consequences would have been disastrous. It is never a good thing to ignore the conviction of the Holy Spirit.

It is God who saves us, and the Holy Spirit who empowers us to overcome sin, and to become more like Jesus Christ in our lives. As individuals, we have free will, and we have the choice to accept or reject Jesus Christ as our Lord and Savior. Once we are born again, we retain our free will to either follow the Lord or not. God does not destroy the free will of humans once we are saved. This is why Christians choose to sin, after they are born again.

When a Christian sins; they are sinning against God and themselves, in the sense that they are sinning against their born again nature. This is why sin is not as appealing or enjoyable as it once was, because it creates conflict within our being, and it creates appropriate guilt and remorse. In addition, the Holy Spirit is convicting the believer regarding their sin.

DARNELL L. SHERMAN MS AMFT

The following is the conclusion of a situation in which our Lord and Savior; Jesus Christ, rescued an adulterous woman from an angry mob.

> *When Jesus had lifted up himself, and saw none but the woman, he said unto her, Woman, where are those thine accusers? hath no man condemned thee? She said, No man, Lord. And Jesus said unto her, Neither do I condemn thee: go, and sin no more. Matthew 8:10-11*

Jesus Christ did not condemn the lady caught in adultery, but he did not tell her to go and continue sinning; he told her to go and sin no more. As Christians we are not to sin; however, if we do, we should ask God to forgive us, and try our best not to sin anymore.

> *There is therefore now no condemnation to them which are in Christ Jesus, who walk not after the flesh, but after the Spirit. Romans 8:1.*

Many preachers quote the aforementioned verse, and leave off the second part of it, which is a conditional requirement for the first part. In order for there to be no condemnation for them which are in Christ Jesus, we have to walk after the Spirit of God, and avoid walking after the flesh. You can't have one part without the other part.

> *For the law of the Spirit of life in Christ Jesus hath made me free from the law of sin and death. For what the law could not do, in that it was weak through the flesh, God sending his own Son in the likeness of sinful flesh, and for sin, condemned sin in the flesh: That the righteousness of the law might be fulfilled in us, who walk not after the flesh, but after the Spirit. For they that are after the flesh do mind the things of the flesh; but they that are after the Spirit the things of the Spirit. For to be carnally minded is death; but to be spiritually minded is life and peace. Because the carnal mind is enmity against God: for it is not subject to the law of God, neither indeed can be. So then they that are in the flesh cannot please God. Romans 8:2-8.*

The Holy Spirit within Christians bears witness to the truth, and sinning with impunity, violating the rights of others with no guilt or remorse, and seeking material gain at the expense of righteousness; is not the truth of God.

For example Sally may appropriately experience guilt and the conviction of the Holy Spirit over committing fornication, and her pastor tells her, no need to feel guilty; you're not under the law; all is well, Sally knows not all is well, and she is right. Sally needs to experience guilt and acknowledge the conviction of the Holy Spirit, ask God to forgive her, ask God to help her not to sin again, and seek a viable strategy to avoid the sin of fornication moving forward.

As healthy believers in Jesus Christ, we can't abandon our first love. We have to stay on the straight and narrow path, we have to bear our cross daily and follow Jesus Christ, we have to deny ourselves sinful pleasures, and we have to allow the light and love of Jesus Christ to shine through us to others. We can't do any of the aforementioned without the help of the Holy Spirit; however, we have to be willing to follow the guidance of the Holy Spirit.

> *Unto the angel of the church of Ephesus write; These things saith he that holdeth the seven stars in his right hand, who walketh in the midst of the seven golden candlesticks; I know thy works, and thy labour, and thy patience, and how thou canst not bear them which are evil: and thou hast tried them which say they are apostles, and are not, and hast found them liars: And hast borne, and hast patience, and for my name's sake hast laboured, and hast not fainted. Nevertheless I have somewhat against thee, because thou hast left thy first love. Remember therefore from whence thou art fallen, and repent, and do the first works; or else I will come unto thee quickly, and will remove thy candlestick out of his place, except thou repent. Revelation 2:1-5*

The Church of Ephesus made some positive choices; however, they made a very bad choice to leave their first love; the love which they had for God. In the scripture God told them to remember from where they fell, repent and to do their first works. God stated, if they failed to do the aforementioned, he would remove their candlestick out of his place; not a good thing.

> *He that overcometh, the same shall be clothed in white raiment; and I will not blot out his name out of the book of life, but I will confess his name before my Father, and before his angels. He that hath an ear, let him hear what the Spirit saith unto the churches. Revelation 3:5*

God states for those who overcome, he will not blot out his name from the book of life. To overcome the world, one's self and the devil requires some effort on the part of the individual, with the help of the Holy Spirit. What of those who choose not to overcome; well, it appears their names will be blotted out of the book of life, and they will spend eternity in hell. This is not rocket science. God's loves us and we can overcome our opposition, with the help of the Holy Spirit. We simply have to choose to follow God's will, seek an intimate and loving relationship with the Lord, and ask the Holy Spirit for help and guidance, and follow it.

Enter ye in at the strait gate: for wide is the gate, and broad is the way, that leadeth to destruction, and many there be which go in thereat: Because strait is the gate, and narrow is the way, which leadeth unto life, and few there be that find it. Matthew 7:13-14

The little progress I have made as a believer in Jesus Christ, is because of the Grace of God and the help of the Holy Spirit. I chose to ask God for help in overcoming sin, and he provided help to me, and I chose to receive the help. I realized I could not keep living a life of sin, if I wanted to please God, and I chose to make a change and seek God's help in helping me to change into a more righteous person. I realize I am not perfect; therefore, while mortal I will always make mistakes; no human on earth is perfect. As a result, I need God to help me to reduce the frequency, intensity and depravity of my sins. I still sin; however, my sins of today are not as depraved as they once were; nor do I sin with the frequency and abandon in which I used to. I thank God for that!

Only the Holy Spirit can help humans overcome sin. There are levels of sin, and some will argue that all sin is the same; I disagree. One who steals a magazine from a store has committed the sin of theft; however, most sane people would realize, that stealing a magazine is not as an egregious of a sin, as committing multiple murders.

So, even though we will never be perfect on the earth, our goals as believers in Jesus Christ, is to move closer to perfection everyday, by gradually reducing the frequency, depravity and intensity of our sin. Only the Holy Spirit can help us complete this task. After realizing we are powerless to overcome sin on our own, we have to choose to ask God for help, we have to choose to receive God's help, by making an effort to sin less, and grow closer to God through praying, reading the Holy Bible, and having healthy relationships with other believers in Jesus Christ.

The Christian life on earth is not easy; we can't sin with impunity, fail to repent and expect to enter heaven. Despite the sunshine, lemonade and rainbow preachers and teachers who never mention the words hell, death, sin or judgment; God wants us to avoid sin and follow his laws and commandments. He is present for us and willing to help us.

It can't be any clearer:

If ye love me, keep my commandments. John 14:15

JALOPY

Riding

Ant hill
Ants
Going in
Coming out
I destroy it

Am I superior to the ants?
I destroyed their home
I killed them
I cannot create them
Do the ants worship me?
Am I king of the ants?

Riding

Brand new Challenger
How long will it last?
Temporary material
Junkyard bound
As they all are in the showroom

We're just passing through
This world is temporary
I am not the king of the ants
I am a servant of Jesus Christ

TWILIGHT JESUS

Purple, blue, orange and white

Clouds

Sailing over mountains

Twilight time

I have left the earth

My spirit is free

Jesus meets me

Smiles and welcomes me home

We embrace

As tears of joy flow

I say, thank you!

APPENDIX A

In America, if you are feeling like ending your life or hurting yourself; please call the national suicide intervention line at 988 or text them at 741741.

The following is a list of additional resources by state. In the time this manuscript was written, and in the time this book was published; it is possible some of the resources may have changed; however, the national suicide intervention line 988 should work and the text line at 741741 twenty-four hours a day, as well as 211 and 911. 211 is a resource line for general help including mental health resources. 911 is a national telephone number for emergency services. Most of the following resources operate twenty-four hours and seven days a week.

American Foundation For Suicide Prevention: https://afsp.org (855) 869-2377.
National Rape, Abuse & Incest Network (RAINN) (800) 656-4673.
Child Abuse Hotline (National) Phone: (800) 252-2873.
Do not kill yourself or harm yourself; you are a very valuable and important person. God loves you!

ALABAMA

Crisis Center of East Alabama (334) 821-8600. The Crisis Center Central Alabama (205) 323-7777. Teen Link (205) 328-LINK (5465). Kids Help Line (205) 328-KIDS (5437).

Senior Talk Line (205) 328-TALK (8255). Teen Crisis Line: (256) 547-9505. Crisis Services of North Alabama (256) 716-1000 or 1-800-691-8426. Family Counseling Center of Mobile, Inc. (251) 431-5111 or 1-800-239-1117

ALASKA

Anchorage Crisis Line; (907) 258-7575 or 1-800-478-7575.
South Central Counseling Center; (907) 563-3200. Fairbanks (907) 452-HELP (4357) 1-877-266-HELP (4357). Kenai Crisis Line (907) 283-7511. Ketchikan Crisis Line; (907) 225-4135. Wasilla Crisis Line (907) 376-2411.

ARIZONA

Arizona Teen Crisis Solutions (623) 879-9600. Alternative Behavioral Services (602) 222-9444 or 1-800-631-1314. TeenLifeline.org (602) 248-TEEN (602) 248-8336 or 1-800-248-TEEN, 1-800-248-8336. Suicide Crisis Hotlines (480) 784-1500 or 1-866-205-5229. ASU Hotline (480) 921-1006. Additional Crisis Lines (520) 622-6000 or 1-800-796-6762.

ARKANSAS

Northwest Arkansas Crisis Intervention Center 1-888-274-7472. Teenline (501) 872-TEEN (8336) or 1-800-798-TEEN (8336). Phone Friend for Kids - 24-hour Warmline for Latchkey Kids 1-888-723-3225 or 1-800-393-9667 – TTY. Community Counseling Services (501) 624-7111 or 1-800-264-2410

CALIFORNIA

Alameda County; 1-800-309-2131 or (510) 792-HELP (4357) Butte County; Adults (530) 891-2810 or 1-800-334-6622; Youth (530) 891-2794 or (800) 371-4373.

Calaveras County; (209) 754-3239 or 1-800-499-4030.

Contra Costa County; 1-800-833-2900; TTD/TTY (925) 938-0725 or 1-888-678-7277. Psychiatric Emergency Services; Placerville (530) 622-3345. South Lake Tahoe; (503) 544-2219.

Garden Grove; (714) 639-4673. For Teens; (714) 639-8336.

Imperial County; (760) 482-4000 or 1-800-817-5292.

Lassen County; 1-888-530-8688.

Los Alamitos; (562) 596-5548 or (714) 894-4242.

Los Angeles County; 1-800-854-7771. Didi Hirsch (310) 391-1253 or

1-877-727-4747. Teens Helping Teens; 1-800-852-8336 or 1-310-855-4673. Foundation for Religious Freedom; 1-800-556-3055.

Marin County; Psychiatric Emergency Services (415) 499-6666 or (415) 499-1100. Grief Counseling (415) 499-1195.

Fort Bragg (707) 964-4747. Ukiah (707) 463-4396. Willits (707) 456-3850. Community Help Line 1-800-575-4357.

Nevada County (530) 265-5811.

Orange County; WarmLine call or text (714) 991-5412 or 1-877-910-9276. Centralized Assessment Team - 1-866-830-6011 www.ochealthinfo.com/CATPERT College Hospital Crisis Response Team - 1-800-773-8001 Available 24 hours https://www.chc. la/cosAdultPsychiatricServices E.T.S Evaluation and Treatment Services - 714-834-6900 24-hour service. UCI Psychiatric Emergency - 714-456-5801 - 24-hour screening service. http://www.ucihealth. org/medical-services/psychiatry Medi-Cal Emergency Access - 1-800-723-8641 - Available 24-hours. http://www.ochealthinfo. com/bhs/about/medi_cal Iris OC- Locally growing healthy lives - 949-238-8093. https://iris-oc.com/service/ Suicide Prevention Lifeline (800) 273-8255. 24 hours Orange County Crisis/Suicide Prevention Hotline (877) 7-CRISIS or (877) 727-4747. ETS: (714) 834-6900. Crisis Line for People with Disabilities: (800)-426-4263. 24-Hrs. Domestic Violence Hotline: (800)-799-7233. Rape Crisis Hotline: (714)-957-2737 24 Hrs. Sexual Assault Victim Services : (714)-834-4317. The OC Warm Line (877) 910-9276. Managed Care Outpatient Services: (800)-723-8641. Children and Youth Services: (714)-834-5015. Child Abuse Registry: (714)-940-1000. Orange County Outreach and Engagement - Adults: (714) 517-6355, Children: (714) 480-4670. OC Behavioral Health Services (855) 625-4657, (714) 834-2332 (TDD)

Placer County; (530) 886-5401. Auburn 1-888-886-5401.

Plumas and Sierra Counties; (530) 283-4333 or 1-877-215-7273.

Riverside County; California Youth Crisis Line; Ages 12-24 - All Youth Issues

24 hours / 7 days; 1-800-843-5200. Helpline of Riverside; (951) 686-4357. (951) 509-2499 or (951) 349-4195.

Sacramento; Auburn (530) 885-2300, Lincoln (916) 645-8866, Roseville (916) 773-3111, Sacramento (916) 368-3111 or (916) 732-3637.

San Bernardino County; 1-800-832-9119. Crisis Walk in Center: High Desert 12240 Hesperia Rd., Victorville, Calif., 92395; (760) 245-8837. Crisis Walk in Center: Morongo Basin 7293 Dumosa Ave., Suite 2, Yucca Valley, Calif., 92884. (855) 365-6558. Community Crisis Response Teams (CCRT) West Valley Office: (909) 458-1517,
Pager: (909) 535-1316. East Valley Office: (909) 421-9233, Pager: (909) 420-0560. High Desert Office: (760) 956-2345, Pager: (760) 734-8093. Morongo Basin (760) 499-4429.
Community Crisis Services Administration; (909) 873-4453.

San Diego County

Access & Crisis Line 1-800-479-3339 or (619) 641-6992 TDD or (888) 724-7240.
San Diego Youth Services: call/text (619) 241-0608.

Cal State Northridge (818) 349-4357.

San Francisco: Friendship Line for the Elderly: 1-800-971-0016
San Francisco: (415) 752-3778. 24-Hour Crisis Hotline (415) 781-0500

Linea Nocturna - Spanish Nightline
8:00 PM to 12:00 AM (415) 989-5212 or 1-800-303-7432.

San Joaquin: Crisis Phone (209) 468-8686

San Jose/Silicon Valley: (408) 279-8228. Teen 1-888-247-7717

San Luis Obispo County: (805) 549-8989 or 1-800-549-8989.
Senior Services (805) 544-0566

San Mateo County: North County (650) 579-0350. South County (650) 368-6655. Coastside (650) 726-6655. Teen Hotline (650) 579-0353.
Santa Barbara County: 1-800-400-1572. Santa Barbara (805) 899-0061

Santa Maria (805) 928-5818. Lompoc (805) 734-2711. Santa Ynez (805) 688-1905.

Santa Clara County: San Jose (408) 279-3312, North County (650) 494-8420, South County (408) 683-2482.

Santa Cruz Counties: 1-877-663-5433, (831) 458-5300 or (831) 649-8008.

Shasta County: (530) 225-5252 or 1-800-821-5252.

Sisklyou County: 1-800-842-8979.

Stanislaus County: (209) 558-4600.

Sutter and Yuba Couties: (530) 673-8255 or 1-888-923-3800.

Ventura County: (805) 652-6727

Yolo County: (530) 756-5000 or 530-756-7542. www.suicidepreventionyolocounty.org West Sacramento (916) 372-6565, Davis (530) 753-0797, Woodland (530) 668-8445, Sacramento (916) 371-3779.

COLORADO

Arvada: (800) 784 2433. Jefferson Center for Mental Health; (303) 425-0300, 1-800-201-5264 or (303) 432-5049 TDD.

Boulder: (303) 447-1665, Colorado Springs: (719) 635-7000 or (719) 596-5433.

Denver: (303) 860-1200, Youth (303) 894-9000. Englewood: (303) 795-6187.

Greeley (970) 353-3686, Fort Collins (970) 221-2114 or After Hours & Weekends

(970) 221-5551. Pueblo: (719) 544-1133. Teen (719) 564-5566

CONNETICUT

Valley Mental Health Services: (203) 736-2601 ext. 370. Branford: (203) 483-2630. Bridgeport: (203) 551-7507. Danbury Hospital: (888) 447-3339. Dayville: (860) 774-2020, Derby; (203) 732-7541 or 1-800-354-3094. East Hartford: (860) 895-3100. Enfield;

(860) 683-8068. Hartford; (860) 297-0999. Samaritans; (860) 232-2121. Manchester; Genesis Center; (860) 747-3434. Meriden; 1-800-567-0902 or (203) 630-5305. Middletown; (860) 344-6496 or RVS (860) 344-2100. Milford; Bridges (203) 878-6365.

New Haven; (203) 974-7735, (203) 974-7713, (203) 974-7300 or (203) 974-7295 (TDD). Youth; 1-888-979-6884. Norwich; (860) 859-9302. Plainville; (860) 747-3434,

(860) 524-1182 or (860) 747-8719. Rocky Hill Dial 211 or 1-800-203-1234. Stamford;

(203) 358-8500. Torrington; (888) 447-3339. Waterbury; (203) 573-6500. West Mystic;

1-800-848-1281 or (860) 848-1281.

DELAWARE

Milford; 1-800-345-6785. Wilmington; 1-800-262-9800, (302)761-9100 or (302)761-9700 TTY. Mobile Crisis Intervention Service; 1-800-652-2929 or (302)577-2484. Brandywine Program Tressler Center of Delaware (302)633-5128.

FLORIDA

Alachua County; (352) 264-6789. Bartow; 1-800-627-5906; Youth Line (863) 519-8011 or 1-877-822-5205. Brevard County Dial 211 or (321) 632-6688. Broward County; (954) 537-0211. Seniors; (954) 390-0485. Teen Hotline; (954) 567-8336. Children; (954) 390-0486. Citrus County; (352) 726-7155. Daytona Beach; 1-800-539-4228. Hillsborough County; (813) 234-1234 or (813) 234-1234 TDD/TTY. Teen Link; (813) 236-8336.

Parent Link; (813) 272-7368; Elder Net Services; (813) 964-1577.

Jacksonville & Duval County; (904) 632-0600 or 1-800-346-6185. Key West; (305) 296-4357. Teen Line (305) 292-8440. Lake County; Christian Volunteer Helpline; (352) 483-2800. Lantana; 211 or (561) 383-1111. Hernando & Pinellas Counties; (727) 562-1542 and (727) 562-1543. Orange & Seminole Counties; (407) 740-7477.

Miami; (305) 358-4357 or (305) 358-2477 TDD/TTY. Teen (305) 377-8336.

Teen Talk Line; (305) 377-8255. Children (305) 358-4357. Marion County;

(352) 629-9595. Okaloosa County; (850) 244-9191. Crestview; (850) 682-0101. Orlando;

(407) 425-2624. Teen Hotline (407) 841-7413. Pensacola; (850) 438-1617, Teen Line;

(850) 433-8336. Pinellas County; (727) 791-3131, (727) 541-4628 or (727) 344-5555.

St. Lucie County; (772) 562-2000. Tallahassee; (850) 224-6333. Parent Helpline;

1-800-352-5683. Children's Mental Health; (850) 224-6333 or 1-877-211-7005.

PhoneFriend - Warmline for Kids; (850) 222-1141; Schools Days 3:00-6:00pm. Christian Helpline Network; 24 hours /7 days; (813) 251-4000. Walton County; (850) 892-4357.

Santa Rosa Beach; (850) 267-2220, 1-800-955-8770 or 1-800-955-8771 TDD.

GEORGIA

Albany; (912) 430-4052 or 1-866-582-7763. Augusta; (706) 560-2943. Brunswick;

(912) 280-1450 or (912) 254-3380. Columbus; (706) 327-3999. DeKalb Coounty;

(404) 892-4646. Dublin; (478) 275-6509. Emanuel County; 1-800-426-5726. Fulton County; (404) 730-1600 or (404) 730-1608 TDD. Lafayette; 1-800-882-1552. Macon;

(478) 751-4484. Marietta; (770) 422-0202. Milldgeville; (478) 445-4357. Paulding County; 1-800-493-1932. Statesboro; (912) 764-5125 or 1-800-746-3526. Thomasville; 1-800-784-2433 or 1-800-662-4357. Waycross; 1-800-342-8168.

HAWAII

Island of Oahu; (808) 832-3100; Islands of Kauai, Lanai, Molokai, Maui, & Hawaii; 1-800-753-6879; AFSP (American Foundation for Suicide Prevention) Hawaii Chapter; (808) 521-6110.

IDAHO

Idaho Statewide; 1-800-564-2120, 211 or 1-800-926-2588. Boise, Valley & Elmore Counties; (208) 334-0808 or 1-800-600-6474. Coeur D'Alene; (208) 769-1406 or

1-888-769-1405. Idaho Falls; 1-800-209-8405 or 1-800-708-3474. Kellogg;

1-888-769-1405. Latah County; (509) 332-1505. Lewiston; 1-800-669-3176. Mountain Home; 1-800-600-6474. McCall Valley Counties; 1-800-600-6474. Pocatello; (208) 233-0590, Teen; 1-800-949-0057. Twin Falls; (208) 734-4000.

ILLINOIS

Statewide - 1-800-322-1431. Adams County; (217) 222-1166. Aurora; (630) 966-9393 or TTY (630) 884-5063. Champaign County; (217) 359-4141. Chicago; (312) 996-5535, (312) 996-3490, or (844) 756-8400 or (833)-626-4244. Christian County; (217) 824-4905 Day Time Emergency/ Crisis after hours; (217) 824-3335 or (217) 824-4905 TDD. DeWitt County; (217) 935-9496. Dupage County; (630) 627-1700. Edgemont; (618) 397-0963 or (618) 397-0961 TTY. Elgin; (847) 697-2380 or (847) 742-4057 TTY. Youth; 1-800-345-9049.

Jefferson County; (618) 242-1512 Hamilton County; (618) 643-4025. Kane County; (630) 482-9696; Lincoln Crisis Clinic; (217) 732-3600. McLean County; (309) 827-5351. McClean County; (309) 827-4005. McHenry County; 1-800-892-8900. Montgomery; 1-800-324-5052. Madison; (618) 465-4388 or (618) 877-0316. Matoon; 1-866-567-2400. Quad-City Area - (309) 779-2999. Moultree; (217) 728-7611. Illinois State University; (309) 438-3655 or 309-438-5489 (TDD). Peoria; (309) 673-7373 or 1-800-784-2433.

Rockford; (815) 636-5000, (815) 636-5005, 1-800-866-3733 or Deaf Contact - (815) 636-5008 TDD. Stephenson County; (815) 233-4357 or

1-888-463-6260. Union County; (618) 833-8551. Joliet - (815) 722-3344. Bolingbrook - (630) 759-4555. Frankfort - (815) 469-6166. Mokena - (708) 479-1399. Morris - (815) 942-6611. New Lennox - (815) 485-7366. Peotone - (708) 258-3333. Wilmington - (815) 476-6969.

INDIANA

Anderson & Muncie; (765) 646-8444 or 1-800-435-9143. Boone County; (765) 482-1599. Hamilton, & Marion Counties; (317) 574-1252 or 1-800-560-4038, (317) 630-7791. Elkhart County; (574) 293-8671, 1-800-808-4357 or TTY - (574) 293-4944. Gibson, Posey, Vanderburgh, & Warrick Counties; (812) 423-7791. Indianapolis; (317) 882-5122 or 1-877-882-5122, (317) 621-5700, 1-800-662-3445, (317) 251-7575. Teens; (317) 255-(8336). Tippecanoe & White Counties; (765) 742-0244 or 1-877-419-1632.
Teen Line (765) 423-1872. First Call Information & Referral; 2-1-1 or (765) 423-CALL (2255). Dearborn, Franklin, Ohio, Ripley, Switzerland, and St. Leon Counties;
(812) 537-1302 or 1-877-849-1248. Madison County; (765) 649-5211. Teen; (765) 608-5400. Elkhart, LaPorte, Marshall, Porter, & St. Joseph Counties; (574) 234-0061 or
1-877-234-0061. Vigo County; 1-812-235-8333.

IOWA

IowaCrisisChat.Org. University of Iowa Crisis Support; (844) 461-5420. Great Rivers; 211, 1-800-362-8255. Boone, Carroll, Greene, & Story Counties; 1-800-830-7009. Cedar Rapids; (319) 362-2174 or 1-800-332-4224. Clinton, Muscatine, & Scott Counties; (563) 421-2975. Dubuque; (563) 588-4016. Johnson County; (319) 351-0140. Sioux City; (712) 252-5000. Waterloo; (319) 233-8484.

KANSAS

Emporia; (620) 343-2626. Garden City; (620) 276-7689. Bourbon County - (620) 223-5030. Neosho County - (620) 431-7890. Anderson County - (785) 448-6806. Allen County - (913) 352-8214. Kansas City; (913) 831-1773, (913) 281-1234. Teen; (913) 281-2299. Lawrence - (785) 841-2345. Baldwin City - 888-899-2345. Children; Lawrence and Eudora - (785) 865-2600, Baldwin - 888-211-5333. Salina; (785) 827-4747. Scott City; (620) 334-5619. Ulysses; (620)

356-3198. Wichita/Sedgwick County; (316) 263-3770, (316) 660-7500 or TTY (800) 766-3777. Wichita State University; 316-978-3440.

KENTUCKY

Ashland; 1-800-562-8909. Bowling Green; 1-800-223-8913. Teen Line; 1-888-837-3964.

Elizabethtown Crisis Line; (270) 769-1304, TDD - 1-888-182-8266. Hopkinsville; 1-877-473-7766. Lexington; 1-800-928-8000. Louisville; (502) 589-4313, 1-800-221-0446, TDD (502) 589-4259 or 1-877-589-4259. Daviess County - (270) 684-9466. Hancock, Henderson, McLean, Ohio, Union, and Webster Counties; 1-800-433-7291. Prestonburg; 1-800-422-1060.

LOUISIANA

Alexandria; (318) 443-2255. Baton Rouge; (225) 924-3900. Outside Baton Rouge 1-800-437-0303 or (225) 437-0303. Beauregard De Ridder Community; (318) 462-0609. Jefferson; (504) 734-2112. Lafayette, Acadiana and beyond; 211 or (337) 232-4357. Leesville; (337) 239-4357. Metairie; (504) 523-2673. Monroe; (318) 387-5683. Y.W.C.A. (318) 323-1505 or 1-800-716-7233. New Orleans; 1-800-366-1740, (504) 269-2673, 1-800-749-2673 or 211. Youth; (504) 895-2550.

MAINE

Statewide; 1-888-568-1112. Bangor Youth Crisis Stabilization Program;
For Ages 6-19; 1-800-499-9130. Biddeford; (207) 284-1087 or 1-888-568-1112. Farmington; (207) 779-2250. Knox County; (207) 594-2490 or 1-888-568-1112. Lewiston; Tri-County Mental Health Services; (207) 783-4680. Washington County;
1-888-568-1112. Ingraham; (207) 774-4357, 1-888-568-1112 or TTY (207) 774-0700. Greater Rumford AMI; 1-800-335-9999. Saco; Counseling Services; (207) 284-1087 or 1-888-568-1112. Child Services; (207) 282-6136 or (207) 774-4357. Skowhegan; (207) 474-2506 or 1-800-452-1933. Children; 1-800-400-2506 or 1-800-621-2552. Waldo County; (207) 338-2295 or 1-888-568-1112. Waterville; (207) 873-2136. York County;
(207) 324-1111.

MARYLAND

Crisis Hotline Statewide; 1-800-422-0009. Baltimore; (410) 521-3800 or (410) 752-2272. Howard County & Central Maryland; (410) 531-6677. TDD Line - Hearing Impaired; (410) 531-5086. Frederick County; (301) 662-2255. Youth Crisis Hotline; (301) 695-5683. Home Alone Phone Friend for Kids; (301) 694-8255. Parent Stress Line; (301) 662-2255. Seniors; (301) 663-0011. Baltimore County; (410) 931-2214. Hyattsville; (301) 864-7130. Maryland Crisis Hotline; 1-800-422-0009 or (301) 864-7161. Prince George's County; (301) 927-4500. Post Partum Depression Hotline; 1-800-1-800-773-6667. Montgomery County; (240) 777-4000 or (240) 777-4815 TTY. Salisbury; (410) 749-4357 or (410) 749-4363.

MASSACHUSETTS

Boston Samaritans Statewide Helpline: (877) 870-4673. Emergency Services Mobile Intervention; 1-877-392-1609 or call 911. Greater Boston Regional Suicide Prevention Coalition www.greaterbostonpreventssuicide.org info@greaterbostonpreventssuicide.org Dial 988 if in crisis. Fall River; (508) 999-7267 or (508) 673-3777. Cape Cod; (508) 548-8900 or 1-800-893-9900. Farmingham: (508) 875-4500 or (877) 870-4673. Teens; 1-800-252-8336. North Essex; (978) 521-7777 or 1-800-281-3223. Holyoke; (413) 536-2251. Merrimack Valley; (978) 688-6607, (978) 452-6733, (978) 372-7200 or (978) 465-6100. Teen; 1-888-767-8336. Northampton; (413) 586-5555 or 1-800-322-0424. Norwood; (781) 769-8674 or 1-800-529-5077. Springfield; (413) 733-6661. Boston Medical Center Psychiatric Services; (617) 979-7028. Westfield; (413) 568-6386.

MICHIGAN

Ann Arbor; (734) 662-2222 or (734) 936-5900. Oakland County; (248) 456-0909 or 1-800-231-1127. Teen 2 Teen Talkline; (248) 292-0194. Macomb County; (586) 307-9100. Coldwater; (517) 279-8404 or (517) 278-2129. Detroit; (313) 224-7000. Veterans; 313-576-1000, ext. 65794. Email: VHASPCMI-553DETSuicidePreventionTeam@va.gov (313) 576-4343 or 313-576-1000, ext. 64249.

Lansing; (517) 337-1717 or (517) 351-4000. Flint; (810) 257-3740. Blue Water; (810) 985-7161 or 1-800-462-6350. Kent County; (616) 336-3535. Holland; (616) 396-4357. East Ottawa County; (616) 458-4357. Grand Haven; (616) 842-4357. Kalamazoo; (269) 381-4357. Lapeer County; (810) 667-0500. Mt. Clemens; (810) 463-6990. Mt. Pleasant; The Listening Ear.com. Isabella County; (989) 772-2918. Clare County; (989) 386-2774, TTY (989) 775-0480. West Michigan; (231) 722-4357 or 1-888-919-7099. Pontiac; 1-800-231-1127, (810) 456-0909 or (810) 456-1919. St. Clair County; 1-810-987-6911 or 1-888-225-4447. Saginaw County; 1-800-233-0022. Cass, Van Buren and South Berrien Counties; 1-800-310-5454. Three Rivers; 1-800-622-3967. Northern Michigan; (231) 922-4800 or 1-800-442-7315. Washtenaw County; (734) 996-4747.

MINNESOTA

Toll-Free Statewide; 1-800-865-0606. Dakota County; (952) 891-7171 or (952) 891-7202 TDD. Brainerd; (218) 828-4357 or 1-800-462-5525. Duluth; (218) 723-0099 or 1-800-720-3334. Grand Rapids/Itasca County; (218) 326-8565, 1-800-442-8565, (218) 326-4634 TTY or 1-800-543-7709. Luverne; 1-800-642-1525, 1-800-642-1525 TDD or (507) 372-7671 TDD. Marshall; (507) 532-3236 or 1-800-658-2429. Minneapolis; (612) 873-2222 or (612) 873-3161. Twin Cities/St. Paul; (612) 379-6363, (612) 379-6377 TDD, or (612) 379-1199. Steele & Waseca Counties; (507) 451-9100 or 1-866-451-9191. Pipestone; 1-800-642-1525. Ramsey County; (651) 266-7900. Regions Hospital Emergency Center; (651) 254-1000 or (651) 254-3285 TDD. Waconia; (952) 442-7601. Washington County; (651) 777-4455 or (612) 379-6377 TDD. Willmar; 1-800-992-1716. Winona; (507) 454-2528, 1-800-362-8255 or 1-800-362-8255 TTY. Worthington; 1-800-642-1525 or 1-800-642-1525 TDD.

MISSISSPPI

Columbus; (662) 328-0200 or (662) 327-4357. Ten Line; (662) 328-4327. Jackson; (601) 713-4357. Resources; (800) 357-0388 or (205) 335-1876. Mental Health Assocation of South Mississippi; (228) 864-6274. Resources; 1-800-985-5990, and you may text TalkWithUs to 66746, or 1-877-210-8513. Additional resources for Mississippians are located at www.

mentalhealthms.com and www.standupms.org. Pike and Warren Counties; 1-601-713-4357. Lowndes County; (662) 328-0200.

MISSOURI

Statewide; 1-800-356-5395 or 1-800-356-5395. Central & Southeast Missouri; 1-888-279-8188 or 1-800-833-3915 or 1-800-395-2132. Eastern Missouri; 1-800-811-4760
TTY for Hearing Impaired, (314) 469-3638 or St. Louis; (314) 469-6644. Joplin/Nevada; 1-800-247-0661. Kennett; 1-800-356-5395. Mexico; 1-800-833-2064. Monett; 1-800-801-4405. Springfield; (417) 862-6555 or 1-800-494-7355. St Louis; Youth under 21; (314) 644-5886 or 1-888-644-5886. St. Louis Adults; (314) 647-4357 or (314) 647-5959 TDD. Western Missouri; 1-888-279-8188 or 1-800-955-8339 TDD.
Missouri Suicide Prevention Network; (573) 634-4626; Aadmin@Mospn.org.

MONTANA

Statewide; 1-800-332-8425. Billings; (406) 252-5658. Bozeman Help Center; (406) 586-3333. Great Falls; (406) 453-4357. Helena; (406) 443-5353. Kalispell; (406) 752-6262 or (406) 752-8181. Resources; (406) 443-7871. Montana Mental Health Association; (888) 268-2743 x406. Montana State University Crisis team number: (406) 259-8800 (Community Crisis Center); MSUB Student Health Services M-F 8:00-5:00; (406) 657-2153. Local mental health agency number: (406) 252-5658 (Mental Health Center)

NEBRASKA

Father Flanagan's Girls and Boys Town.org Original; (800) 448-3000 or TTY (800) 448-1833. Lincoln; (402) 441-7940 or 1-800-464-0258. Crisis Line; (402) 379-3798 or (877) 379-3798. Catholic Charities; Office (402) 558-5700 or Crisis; (402) 558-5700. Grand Island; (3080 381-0555 or (866) 995-4422. Hope Crisis Center; Crisis: (877) 388-4673.
Parent Child Center; (308) 324-3040, (800) 215-3040 or Spanish (308) 324-1942 or (866) 351-9594. Sand Hills Crisis Intervention Program; Crisis: 308-284-6055. Rural Domestic Violence Program; (402) 922-3712 or (844) 299-9612. Nebraska Family Helpline; (888) 866-8660. Doves Crisis Lines: Gering; (866) 953-6837, Lincoln; (402) 437-9302, North Platte; (888) 534-3495.

NEVADA

Las Vegas Suicide Prevention Center; (702) 456-0244. Reno; (800) 992-5757 or (775) 784-8090. All of Nevada; (877) 885-4673, (800) 273-8255 or Text; 839863. Sexual Assault Hotline: (775) 221-7600. Self-Injury Hotline; (800) 366-8288). Poison Information; (702) 732-4989. Poison Control (Clark County) (888) 446-6179 or (800) 222-1222. Rape Crisis Hotline (Las Vegas) (702) 366-1640 or TTD (702) 385-4979. Runaway Hotline Las Vegas; (800) 621-4000. Suicide Prevention Center of Clark County; (702) 731-2990. Suicide Prevention Nevada; (877) 885-4673. Youth Runaway Emergency Shelter Las Vegas; (702) 385-3330. Alcoholics Anonymous (AA) (702) 598-1888. Child Abuse Hotline Clark County; (702) 399-0081. Child Protective Services Clark County; (702) 455-0000. Crisis Mental Health Unit; (702) 486-8020. Domestic Violence Shelter Las Vegas; (702) 646-4981. Domestic Violence Hotline; (800) 799-7233. Gamblers Anonymous Hotline; (888) 442-2110 or (800) 522-4700.

NEW HAMPSHIRE

New Hampshire Help Line; (603) 225-9000 or (800) 852-3388. Merrimack & Surrounding Counties; (603) 226-0817 or (800) 852-3323. The Samaritans of the Monadnock Region; (603) 357-5505 or (603) 924-7000. Teen Hotline; (877) 583-8336. New Hampshire & Vermont; (603) 448-4400. Teen line; (800) 639-6095. Manchester; (603) 668-4111. Nashua; (800) 762-8191 or TDD (800) 735-2964. UNH; (800) 273-8255 or Text WILDCAT to 741741.

NEW JERSEY

Atlantic City: Crisis Hotline; (609) 344-1118. Guidance Center; (856) 455-5555 or (856) 455-7621 TTY. Burlington County; (856) 234-8888, (856) 234-3451, (609) 267-8500 or (609) 871-4700. Teen Line; (856) 234-0634 or (609) 871-1433. Cherry Hill; (856) 795-2155 or (877) 266-8222. Teen Line; (856) 795-2119 or (888) 375-8336. St. Mary's Hospital Community Mental Health Center; (201) 795-5505. Hunterdon Helpline; (800) 272-4630 or (908) 782-4357. Comprehensive Behavioral Healthcare; (201) 935-3322, (201) 646-0333 or (201) 262-4357. Mercer County; (609) 896-2120 or (609) 585-2244. Teen line; (609) 896-4434. Montclair; (973) 744-6522. Morristown; (973) 540-0100. Burlington; (609) 261-8000. Newark; (973) 623-2323. Ocean County;

(732) 240-6100, (609) 693-5834 or (800) 245-9090. Northern New Jersey; (973) 831-1870, (973) 831-1871 or (888) 904-1700. Riverview Medical Center; (732) 219-5325 or We Care 24-Hour Crisis Hotline; (908) 232-2880.

NEW MEXICO

Albuquerque: Agora Crisis Center; (505) 277-3013. Toll-free Statewide (866) 435-7166. Portales; 1-800-432-2159. Family Violence Prevention Team IHS Mental Health; (505) 837-4245. Crisis Response of Santa Fe; (505) 820-6333 or (888) 920-6333. New Mexico Crisis Line; (855) 662-7474. Peer to Peer Warm Line; (855) 466-7100. First responder Support Line; (855) 507-5509.

NEW YORK

Albany: Capital District Psychiatric Center; (518) 447-9650. The Samaritans Suicide Prevention Center; (518) 689-4673. Allegany; Counseling Center; (716) 593-5706; Teen Hotline; (888) 448-3367. Batavia; (585) 343-1212 or (800) 359-5727. Orleans County; (585) 345-9406 or (800) 889-1903. Wyoming County; (585) 343-2942 or (800) 786-3300. Long Island Crisis Center; (516) 679-1111. Buffalo; (716) 834-3131; Kids Helpline (716) 834-1144 or Toll-Free; (800) 543-7400. Essex & Franklin Counties; (518) 561-2330. Dutchess County; (845) 485-9700 or (877) 485-9700. Ellenville; (845) 647-2443. Jamestown; (716) 484-1314 or (315) 782-2327. New Paltz; (845) 255-8801 or (845) 257-2920. Oasis Peer Counseling; (845) 257-4945.

New York; New York; The Samaritans; (212) 673-3000 or (212) 532-2400. Niagra County Crisis Hotline; (716) 285-3515. Orange County; (8880 750-2266, (845) 294-9355 or (800) 832-1200. Rochester; (585) 275-5151, (800) 310-1160, (585) 275-2700 TTY. St. Lawrence County; (315) 265-2422. Suffolk County; (631) 751-7500. Central New York; (315) 251-0600. Cayuga County; (8770 400-8740. Tompkins County; (607) 272-1616. Utica; (315) 734-3456. Westchester; (914) 493-7075, (914) 347-6400. Woodstock; (845) 679-2485 or (845) 338-2370. Yates Youth Services; (315) 536-9979.

NORTH CAROLINA

Ahoskie; (252) 332-4442. Alamance/Caswell; (336) 513-4444 or (252) 247-3023. Chapel Hill; (800) 233-6834. Charlotte; (704) 377-0602, (800) 367-7287. Fayetteville; (910) 485-4134. Durham Center; (800) 510-9132. Elkin; (888) 235-4673. Greensboro; (336) 387-6161. Roanoke Rapids Crisis Line; (252) 537-2909. Johnston County; (919) 934-6161. Teen Line; (919) 934-6162. Manteo; (252) 473-3366. Pitt County; (252) 758-4357. Dial-A-Teen; (252) 758-1976 or (252) 758-4357 TTY. Raleigh Crisis Line; (919) 231-4525 or (800) 844-7410. Teen Talkline; (919) 231-3626. Randolph; (336) 629-0313. Rowan; (704) 633-3616 or (919) 774-4520. Iredell; (704) 872-7638. Mooresville; (704) 664-4357. Wayne County; (919) 735-4357. Wilmington; (910) 392-7408 or (800) 672-2903, (252) 237-5156. Teen Help Line; (252) 243-6444. Winston-Salem; (336) 723-4338 or (336)722-5153. Teen Line (336) 723-8336.

NORTH DAKOTA

Bismark; (701) 328-8889, (888) 328-2112, (800) 472-2911. Fargo; (701) 232-4357.
Grand Forks; (701) 775-0525, (701)328-8736, (701) 328-8920 or (701)328-8736.
Focus Family Services; (401)-341-4216. Bismarck Crisis Line; (701) 328-8888 or
(888) 328-2112. First Link 24 Hour Hotline (800) 273-8255. Mental Health Association of North Dakota; 24 hours/7 days; 211 or (800) 472-2911. Youth Works Crisis Line;
(701) 255-6909. Lake Region Human Service Center; (701) 662-5050 (collect calls accepted) or (701) 665-2200. Dickson; (701) 227-7500, (888) 227-7525 or (701) 227-5009. Fargo; 211 or (701) 235-7335, (701) 232-4357 or (800) 273-8255. New Life Center/Shelter; (701) 235-4453. South East Human Service Center; (701) 298-4500,
888) 342-4900 or (701) 235-7335. Youth Crisis Line; (701) 232-8558. Grand Forks;
(701) 775-0525. Rescue Mission; (701) 772-6609, 420-424 Division Avenue
Grand Forks, ND. 58206-6323.

OHIO

Akron; Portage Path Community Mental Health Center; (330) 434-9144 or
(330) 762-6110. Athens; Counseling Services; (740) 593-3344. Teen Line
(800) 222-8336 or (800) 475-8484. Athens; (419) 352-1545 or (800) 472-9411. Bucyrus;
(419) 562-9010, (419) 468-9081 or (800) 755-9010. Canton; (330) 452-6000, (800) 956-6630. Chillicothe Crisis Center; (740) 773-4357. Teen Line; (740) 773-0959. Cincinnati;

Crisis Care Center; (513) 281-2273. Mobile Crisis Team; (513) 584-5098. Psychiatric Emergency Services (PES); (513) 584-8577. Talbert House; Crisis hotline (513) 281-2273 or Text Talbert to 839863. Mental Health Access Point; (513) 558-8888. Cleveland; Crisis Intervention & Referral Service Open Every Night from 8pm to Midnight; (216) 721-1115. Free Crisis Services; (216) 251-7722. Columbus Suicide Hotline; (614) 221-5445. Teen Suicide Hotline; (614) 294-3300. Senior Hotline; (614) 294-3309, TTY (614) 221-5445. Dayton; Suicide Prevention Center; (800) 320-4357, (937) 229-7777 or (937) 463-2961. Delaware & Morrow Counties; (740) 369-3316, (419) 947-2520 or (800) 684-2324.

Serving Gallia, Jackson & Meigs Counties; (800) 252-5554. Kent; (330) 678-4357, (330) 296-3255 or (330) 296-2255 TTY. Lancaster; (740) 687-0500. Lima; (800) 567- 4673 or (419) 227-8443. Mansfield; (419) 522-4357. Marion; (740) 383-2273. Medina; (330) 725-9195. Delaware & Morrow Counties; (740) 369-3316, (419) 947-2520 or (800) 684-2324. Napoleon; (800) 468-4357. Teen Line; (877) 419-7233. New Philadelphia; (330) 627-5240 or (330) 343-1811. Newark; (740) 345-4357 or (800) 544-1601. Community Counseling Crisis Center 24 hours/7 days; (513) 424-5498, (513) 523-4149 or (513) 894-7002. Teen Line; (513) 418-6423 x359. Portage; Emergency Crisis Service (330) 296-3555 or (877) 796-3555.

Toledo; Mental Health Services; (419) 255-9585. Community Connection; (330) 393-1565, (330) 545-4371, (330) 395-8764 or TTY (330) 395-5832. Champaign Counties; (800) 224-0422. Warren & Clinton Counties; (800) 932-3366. Xenia; TCN Behavioral Health Services; (937) 376-8701 or (937) 426-2302.

Youngstown; Help Hotline Crisis Center; (330) 747-2696, (330) 424-7767 or (800) 344-5818, TDD (330) 744-0579. Latchkey Kid Warmline 2:30pm to 6:00pm Mahoning County; (330) 747-5437. Columbiana County; (800) 427-3622, Senior Line; (330) 747-5437. Mental Health Services; (330) 424-7767 or (800) 344-5818. Zanesville; (740) 453-5818, (740) 455-4142 TDD, All Other Areas; (800) 344-5818 or (800) 432-4142 TDD.

OKLAHOMA

Oklahoma Department of Mental Health Crisis Line; (800) 522-9054. United Way Helpline; (580) 355-7575. HeartLine; (405) 848-2273. Helpline; (580) 765-5551. Tulsa

(918) 836-4357. Suicide Prevention Oklahoma; (312) 402-2006. Choctaw and Cimarron Counties; (800) 522-7233. Kiowa Teen Suicide Prevention; (405) 247-5200 or (580) 351-7697. Kiowa Alcohol and Drug Abuse Program; (405) 247-9009 or (405)247-2579. Youth Shelter; (405) 282-7045. United Way Helpline; (580) 355-7575. Newcastle Care Crisis Hotline; (405) 392-2589. Oklahoma City; Suicide Prevention Hotline (800) 273-8255 or (405) 848-2273. Crisis Line; (800) 522-8100 or (800) 522-9054. Oklahoma Department of Mental Health; (800) 535-2437 or (800) 522-9054. Teen Line; (800) 522-8336. OKC Indian Clinic; (405) 948-4900. Youth Crisis; (800) 448-4663 or (918) 582-0061. Teenline; (800) 522-8336. Youth Services; (405) 235-7537. Osage Nation Crisis Line; (866) 897-4747, (918) 287-5422 or (918) 287-5335. Ponca City; (580) 765-5551 or
(580) 762-3603. Sac and Fox Nation; (800) 404-3189 or (918) 968-3901. Seneca/Cayuga Nation; (918) 787-5452 ext. 36. Tahlequah Crisis Hotline; (800) 300-5321 or (918) 456-0673. Tulsa Helpline; (918) 836-4357. Oklahoma University Advocates; (405) 615-0013, Women's Resource Center; (405) 701-5540, Crisis Line; (405) 701-5660.

OREGON

Albany; (800) 560-5535. Hot Springs; (501) 624-7111 or (800) 264-2410. Astoria;
(503) 325-5724. Baker County; (541) 523-5903. Deschutes County Mental Health;
(888) 232-7192. Harney County; (541) 573-8376. Corvallis; (541) 766-6844 or (888) 232-7192 or (541) 758-3000. Polk County; (503) 581-5535. Wallowa County;
(541) 426-3111. Eugene; (541) 687-4000 or (800) 422-7558. Curry County; (877) 519-9322. Grants Pass; (541) 479-4357, (800) 640-0154 or (541) 474-5365. Hillsboro; (503) 291-9111, (541) 575-0030. Klamath County; (541) 882-7291. Union County; (541) 962-8800. Jefferson County; (888) 232-7192. Benton County; (503) 655-8401.
Yamhill County; (503) 434-7465 or (800) 560-5535. Salem; (503) 585-4949. Medford;
(541) 779-4357 or (541) 774-8201. Lincoln County; (888) 232-7192. Coos County; (541) 756-8601. Malheur County; (541) 889-9167. Umatilla County; (541) 278-5720 or (800) 452-5413. Portland/Multnomah Counties; (503) 988-4888 or (800) 716-9769. Pineville; (888) 232-7192, (541) 447-7441 or (541) 447-7960. Douglas County; (541) 440-3532.
Salem; (800) 560-5535, (503) 581-5535, (503) 588-5821 or (503) 585-4949. Columbia County; (503) 397-5211. Dalles; (541) 296-6307, (888) 877-9147. Tillamook County;
(503) 842-8201. Oregon State University; (800) 273-8255.

PENNSYLVANIA

Carlisle; (717) 249-6226. Harrisburg; (717) 652-4400. Adams, Franklin, Perry, Upper Dauphin; (800) 932-4616. Allegheny County; (888) 424-2287. Altoona; (814) 889-2279, (800) 540-4690 or (814) 946-9050. Beaver County; (724) 728-3650 or Ambridge Callers (724) 375-7693. Greater Philadelphia; (215) 355-6000, (215) 547-1889, (215) 340-1998, (215) 536-0911, (215) 686-4420, (610) 649-5250, (888) 855-5525, (724) 287-0440, (800) 292-3866. Holy Spirit Hospital; (717) 763-2345 or (800) 722-5385. Centre County; (800) 643-5432. Chester County; (610) 918-2100 or (877) 918-2100. Dauphin County; (717) 232-7511. Erie Hotline; (814) 453-5656. Hanover; (717) 637-7633, (717) 334-0468 or (866) 325-0339. Lancaster County; (717) 394-2631 or (717) 299-4855.

Adamstown Areas; (717) 738-0738. Hensel; (717) 786-5444. Teen Line; (717) 394-2000, TTY; (717) 299-7184. Lebanon County; (717) 274-3363. Lehigh County; (610) 782-3127. Luzerne/Wyoming Counties; (570) 836-3118, (570) 552-6000, (570) 455-6385, (570) 735-7590. Lawrence County; (724) 658-5529, Teen Line; (724) 657-8255. Montgomery County; (610) 279-6100 or (800) 452-4189. Northampton County; (610) 252-9060 or (610) 997-5840 TTY.

Pittsburgh/Surrounding Areas; (412) 820-4357, (412) 820-4357, (800) 643-5432, (814) 863-0395, (814) 235-1890, (610) 447-7600, (800) 836-6010, (800) 222-8848, (570) 829-1341 or (888) 829-1341. York Hospital Crisis Intervention; (717) 851-5320 or (800) 673-2496. Penn State; (877) 229-6400, Text the 24/7 Crisis Text Line: Text "LIONS" to 741741, or (814) 234-6110.

RHODE ISLAND

Rhode Island Suicide Prevention; (800) 749-3197. Hope Valley; (401) 539-7474. Providence Samaritans; (401) 272-4044 or (800) 365-4044. Sympatico; (401) 783-0782 or (917) 920-0639. University of Rhode Island Health Services; (401) 874-2246.

SOUTH CAROLINA

Toll Free Statewide; (800) 922-2283, Teen Line; (843) 747-8336 or (800) 273-8255. Aiken County; (803) 648-9900. Anderson Crisis Ministries; (864) 226-0297, (864) 868-4878.

Columbia; 211, (803) 790-4357, (803) 733-5408, (866) 892-9211, (864) 487-4357. Greenville; (864) 271-8888, (864) 582-1100, Teen Line; (864) 467-8336. Charleston; (843) 744-4357.

SOUTH DAKOTA

Sioux Falls; (605) 339-8599, (605) 339-4357, (800) 273-8255 or (605) 338-4880. Outside Sioux Falls (888) 378-7398. Rural South Dakota; (800) 664-1349. Farm and Rural Stress Hotline; (800) 691-4336 or (800) 365- 4044.

TENNESSEE

Athens; Helpline (423) 745-9111. Monroe County; (423) 337-3800. Chattanooga; (423) 552-4636, (423) 622-5193, (423) 266-4862. Montgomery County; (931) 648-1000. Woodbridge Hospital; (877) 928-9062. Carter, Greene, Unicoi & Washington Counties; (423) 926-0144, (423) 783-0090. Kingsport; (423) 246-2273. Knoxville; Helen Ross McNabb Center Adult Services (865) 637-9711, Youth Services (865) 523-8695. Knoxville; (865) 523-9124. Teen Line; (865) 523-9124. Elderly; (865) 523-9108
Overlook Mobile Crisis Unit; (865) 539-2409. Memphis; (901) 274-7477. Nashville; Davidson County; (615) 726-0125. Nashville; (615) 244-7444, (800) 681-7444.
Oakridge; (865) 482-4949, TeleFriend; (865) 481-3333. Bedford County; (931) 684-7133. Coffee County; (931) 455-7133. Franklin County; (931) 967-7133. Moore County; (931) 759-7133. Teen Crisis Line; (800) 454-8336. Memphis; (901) 448-2802, (901) 320-1313. All of Tennessee; (855) 274-7471.

TEXAS

Abilene; (325) 677-7773, (800) 758-3344. Amarillo; (806) 359-6699, (800) 692-4039. Austin; (512) 472-4357, (512) 703-1395 TTY. Beaumont; (409) 835-3355, (800) 793-2273. West Texas Centers for Mental Health; (800) 375-4357. Cleburne; (800) 451-1659.
Conroe; (800) 659-6994. Dallas; (214) 330-7722, (214) 828-1000, (972) 233-2233, Teen; (972) 233-8336. Denton County; (800) 762-0157. (800) 269-6233 TTY. El Paso; (915) 779-1800, (877) 562-6467. Houston; (713) 970-7000, (866) 970-4770, (713) 970-7070, (713) 468-5463, Teenline; (713) 529-8336. Longview; (800) 832-1009. Lubbock; (806) 765-8393, (806) 740-1414, (800) 687-7581, TeenLine; (806) 765-7272. Midland; (432) 570-3300. Odessa; (432) 333-3265. Ft. Stockton; (877) 475-7322. Alpine; (800) 542-4005. Roundrock;

(800) 841-1255. San Angelo; (325) 653-5933, (800) 375-8965. San Antonio; (210) 223-7233, (800) 316-9241. Wichita Falls; (800) 621-8504.

UTAH

Ogden; (801) 625-3700. Crisis Line of Utah County; (801) 226-4433. Provo; (801) 373-7393. Salt Lake; (801) 261-1442, (888) 222-2542. National Hotlines; Dial 988, (800) 784-2433 or text 741741.

VERMONT

Brattleboro; (802) 257-7989. Washington County; (802) 229-0591. Clara Martin Center Crisis Line; (800) 639-6360. Addison County; (800) 388-7641. Howard Center Crisis Line; (802) 488-7777. Lamoille County; (802) 888-8888, (802) 888-5026. Northwestern Counseling; (802) 524-6554. Northeast Crisis Line; (802) 334-6744 or (802) 748-3181. Pathways; call or text (833) 888-2557. Rutland Crisis Line; (802) 775-1000. Manchester; (802) 362-3950. Bennington; (802) 442-5491. Washington County; (802) 229-0591 or (800) 622-4235.

VIRGINIA

Washington; (703) 527-4077. Blacksburg; (540) 961-8400. Bristol; (540) 628-7731 or (540) 466-2312. Charlottesville; (804) 295-8255. Danville Area; (804) 792-4357. Dumfries; (703) 368-4141, Teenline (703) 368-8069, Spanish (703) 368-6544. Lynchburg; (804) 947-4357, (888) 947-9747. Martinsville/Henry Counties; (540) 632-7295. Franklin County; (540) 489-5490, Patrick County; (540) 694-2962, Teenline (540) 634-5005. Norfolk; (757) 622-1126. Richmond; (804) 819-4100, Roanoke; (540) 344-1948, Teenline; (540) 982-8336. Clarke County; (540) 667-0145. Frederick County; (540) 667-0145. Page County; (540) 743-3733. Shenandoah County; (540) 459-4742. Warren County; (540) 635-4357. Winchester; (540) 667-0145.

WASHINGTON

Bremerton; (360) 479-3033 or (800) 843-4793. East Clallam County; (360) 452-4500 or (360) 374-6177. Jefferson County; (360) 385-0321 or (800) 659-0321. Wahkiakum County; (800) 635-5985 or (800) 627-2211. Chehalis; (360) 748-6601, (800) 244-7414 or

(360) 748-6696. Asotin/Garfield Counties; (509) 758-3341. Stevens County; (509) 684-4597 or (800) 767-6081. Western Washington; (425) 258-4357 or (800) 584-3578, (800) 846-8517 TTY. Lincoln County; (509) 725-3001 or (800) 767-6081. Columbia County; (509) 382-2527. Ellensburg; (509) 925-4168, (509) 674-2881 or (800) 584-3578. Everett; (425) 258-4357 or (800) 584-3578. Friday Harbor; (800) 584-3578. Hoquiam; (360) 532-4357 or (800) 685-6556. Benton/Franklin Counties; (509) 783-0500 or (800) 548-8761.

Long View; (800) 884-2298 or (360) 425-6064. Moses Lake; (509) 765-1717. Mt. Vernon; (800) 726-6050. Newport; (800) 404-5151. Olympia; (360) 586-2800 or Teen; (360) 586-2777 or (800) 627-2211. Okanogan County; (509) 826-6191. Othello; (509) 659-4357 or (509) 488-5611. Point Angeles; (360) 452-4500. Point Townsend; (360) 385-0321 or (800) 659-0321. Pullman; (509) 332-1505. Ferry County; (800) 269-2380. Richland; (509) 943-6606, Teen Line; (509) 946-8336. Seattle; (206) 224-2840, (206) 461-3614, (206) 461-3222, Teen Line; (206) 461-4922. Kids; (206) 915-7803. Spokane; (509) 838-4428. Skamania County; (509) 427-9488. Tacoma; (253) 272-9882. Clark County; (360) 696-9560, (360) 696-1925 TDD or (800) 626-8137. Walla Walla; (509) 522-4278. Wenatchee; (360) 662-7105 or (509) 662-7105. Palouse Regional Crisis Line; (509) 332-1505. Yakima; (509) 575-4200 or (800) 572-8122.

WASHINGTON D.C.

Washington Metropolitan Area; (703) 527-4077, (888) 793-4357, (202) 673-9319, (703) 746-3401, (703) 228-5160, (540) 825-5656 or (202) 673-9319.

WEST VIRGINIA

Clarksburg; (800) 786-6480. Potomac Highlands; (800) 545-4357. Huntington; (800) 642-3434. Lewisburg; (304) 647-7911 or (800) 232-0020. Statewide; (844) 435-7498 or text (877) 435-7304.

WISCONSIN

Outagamie County; (920) 832-4646 TTY Accessible. Ozaukee County; (262) 377-2673, Teenline; (262) 377-7786, Senior Support Line; (262) 377-7786. Walworth County; (262) 741-3200, (800) 365-1587 or (262) 741-3255 TTY. Fond Du Lac County; (920) 929-3535 or (920)

929-3443 TDD. Green Bay; (920) 436-8888. Kenosha; (262) 657-7188 or (800) 236-7188. La Crosse; (608) 775-4344 or (800) 362-8255. Madison; (608) 280-2600. Milwaukee County; (414) 257-7222 or (414) 257-6300 TDD. Oshkosh; (920) 233-7707. Racine; (262) 637-9557. Rhinelander; (888) 299-1188. Sturgeon Bay; (920) 743-8818 or (800) 914-3571. Waukesha County; (262) 547-3388. Wausau; (715) 845-4326, (800) 799-0122 or (715) 845-4928 TDD. Wisconsin Rapids; (715) 421-2345. Marshfield; (715) 384-5555. University of Wisconsin; (608) 265-5600 ext. 9.

WYOMING

Statewide; (800) 457-9312. Worland; (307) 347-4991. American Foundation for Suicide Prevention; (406) 531-4728. Statewide 24/7- 988. Riverton; (307) 856-8586. Cheyenne; (307) 632-9362 or (307) 634-9653. Douglas; (307) 358-2846. Cody (307) 587-2197. Wellspring; (307) 864-3138. Rawlins; (307) 324-7156. Sheridan; (307) 674-4405.

VETERANS

Veterans Crisis Line; (800)-273-8255 ext. 1. National Coalition for Homeless Veterans; (877) 424-3838. National Organization of Veterans' Advocates; (202) 587-5708.

To anyone who serves and or served America; thank you and may our Lord and Savior; Jesus Christ bless and keep you.

CLOUDS OF WRATH

Moving in
From the Northwest

Nowhere to run
Nowhere to hide

Everyone sees
Everyone fears

Slowing moving towards
Nothing anyone may do

Comments protests and boycotts
All futile
Political statements, interfaith council, religious unity
All futile wastes of time

Destruction is imminent
Unsaved made their choice
Destruction is upon the world

Clouds dark ominous billowing turmoil
Are moving in
The unrighteous cannot escape God's wrath

Biblical Quotes culled from the King James Version of the Holy Bible. KJV; *Cornerstone Family Bible (Nashville, Tennessee, Holman Bible Publishers, 2001).*

Previous works by Darnell L. Sherman:

Life on Planet X: Christ our Salvation. (Bloomington, Indiana: Balboa Press, 2017).

Arcangel808: My Struggle to Know and Serve Jesus Christ. (Bloomington, Indiana: Westbow Press, 2012).

I, Eternal: Poetry and Essay from the Struggle of Existence. (Enumclaw, Washington: Winepress Publishing, 2008).

We Live Eternal. (Lima, Ohio: Fairway Press, 1996).

Onplanetx.com

To my brothers and sisters through the hard times never give up; place your trust in our Lord and Savior, Jesus Christ. Never commit suicide. May God bless you, comfort you, protect you and keep you! See you heaven! Darnell

ABOUT THE AUTHOR

Darnell Sherman is a psychotherapist (Associate Marriage and Family Therapist) practicing in Southern California. He has over twenty-five years of experience treating individuals suffering from major depressive disorders and other psychological disorders. He has also worked exstensively with child abuse and neglect victims.

Darnell is a Christian, and his primary obligation is to his Lord and Savior; Jesus Christ. Darnell earned a Masters in Counseling Psychology from the California State University at Fullerton.

In the tradition of the Danish Philosopher, Soren Kieerkegaard, Darnell views the problems of human existence in terms of a struggle to discover meaning in one's life. Darnell believes the ultimate meaning anyone may achieve is found in a personal relationship with Jesus Christ, which not only transcends this mortal existence, but also transcends all of eternity.

ABOUT THE BOOK

According to the Center for Disease Control, there were 49,449 reported suicide deaths in 2022, in America; the highest total ever. There has been over 30% increase in suicides in America since 2001.

According to the American Foundation for Suicide Prevention, in 2021 there were over 3,500 reported suicides per month in the United States; that is a record high. In 2021 suicide was the second leading cause of death for individuals between 10 and 34 years of age. It appears the Covid-19 pandemic is being replaced with a pandemic of hopelessness. The Anti-Suicide Book for Christians explores how individuals and especially Christians, may find meaning in suffering, and experience a fellowship with Jesus Christ in his suffering and resurrection, and embrace the truth, and a life saving faith which transcends this mortal existence.